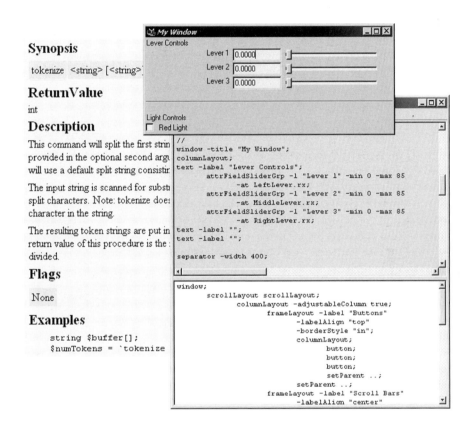

Synopsis

tokenize <string> [<string>]

Return Value

int

Description

This command will split the first strin
provided in the optional second argu
will use a default split string consisti

The input string is scanned for substi
split characters. Note: tokenize does
character in the string.

The resulting token strings are put in
return value of this procedure is the
divided.

Flags

None

Examples

```
string $buffer[];
$numTokens = `tokenize
```

```
//
window -title "My Window";
columnLayout;
text -label "Lever Controls";
        attrFieldSliderGrp -l "Lever 1" -min 0 -max 85
                -at LeftLever.rx;
        attrFieldSliderGrp -l "Lever 2" -min 0 -max 85
                -at MiddleLever.rx;
        attrFieldSliderGrp -l "Lever 3" -min 0 -max 85
                -at RightLever.rx;
text -label "";
text -label "";

separator -width 400;
```

```
window;
        scrollLayout scrollLayout;
                columnLayout -adjustableColumn true;
                        frameLayout -label "Buttons"
                                -labelAlign "top"
                                -borderStyle "in";
                        columnLayout;
                                button;
                                button;
                                button;
                                setParent ..;
                        setParent ..;
                frameLayout -label "Scroll Bars"
                                -labelAlign "center"
```

MEL™ Fundamentals

Alias|Wavefront™

Learning Maya 5 | MEL Fundamentals

Credits:

Glen R. Chang, Shawn Dunn, Marc-André Guindon, Andrew Harris, Bret Hughes, Cory Mogk, John Patton, Eric Saindon

Special Thanks:

Roark Andrade, Tim H. Brown, Steve Christov, Erica Fyvie, Corban Gossett, Deion Green, Bob Gundu, David Haapalehto, Rachael Jackson, Danielle Lamothe, Julio Lopez, Robert MacGregor, Tim McIlravey, Jason Schleifer, Carla Sharkey, Michael Stamler, Marcus Tateishi

Printed in Canada.

MEL-M5-01

ALIAS | WAVEFRONT · 210 KING STREET EAST · TORONTO, ONTARIO · M5A 1J7

MEL Fundamentals

MEL Fundamentals

Following is a brief overview of the content of this book and a section explaining how to install the support files from the included CD.

WHAT IS MEL?

MEL™ stands for Maya Embedded Language. It is a language designed specifically for giving instructions to Maya®. You can use it to automate tasks, customize Maya, create expressions or build scripts that will extend Maya's existing functionality.

Overview

Through a series of real world problem solving examples, workflow enhancements, and applications of MEL into integrated scenes, the MEL Fundamentals book shows you why and how to use MEL. Lectures combine examples of work with and without MEL to show how MEL can simplify the workflow and facilitate complex or tedious tasks.

Examples of what MEL can be used for and how it can save time in your daily workflow:

Create custom dynamic effects

Write scripts that can be used repeatedly as *macros*

Customize the interface to meet your requirements

Quickly enter a command when it is faster than using the corresponding UI

Enter exact values for creating or manipulating scene objects

Execute an action without changing the current UI settings

Set defaults not included in preference settings

Customize Maya specifically for a certain scene or workflow

Create your own commands

Objectives:

- How to customize your Maya environment using MEL This includes hotkeys, marking menus, and shelves

- How to understand and work with attributes

- How to build custom user interface elements using MEL

- How to use expressions to add control to your animations

- How to create and use MEL procedures in scripts, utilities, and other files

Prerequisites

In order to get the most out of this book, it is important to complete the following:

- Complete the *Learning Maya™ 5 | Foundation* tutorials—especially Lesson 25, *Blinking using MEL*

- Reading the MEL documentation will allow students to get much more value from this book

- Read the documentation on Expressions

Concepts

Introduction to MEL

- What is MEL?

- Customizing Maya with MEL

- Shelf buttons, marking menus, hotkeys

Using MEL to access attributes

- Getting and setting attributes values

- Connecting and creating attributes

Creating UI elements

- Windows, Buttons, layouts, widgets

Scripting Basics

- Commands and Syntax

- Explanation of C, E and Q

- General syntax rules for MEL
- Variables

Programming Structures

- Conditional statements - `if`, `else`, `else if`
- Looping statements - `for`, for-in
- Logical operators

Expressions

- Expressions vs. MEL
- Expression syntax
- Function examples

Procedures

- What procedures can do for you
- Creating procedures
- Using procedures in script files

Script files

- What are script files?
- Script files vs. procedures
- Creating and using script files
- Sharing script files

Script Jobs and Script Nodes

- What is a script job?
- How to start and stop script job processes
- Applications of script jobs
- What are script nodes?
- Application of a script node

Appendix

- UI examples
- Expression examples

Installing the data

The directory *MEL_Fundamentals_DATA* on the included CD, contains all the data you need to use this product. This folder is just like a *maya* folder, with a different name.

Installing the MEL Fundamentals data

1 Locate your maya folder

- For IRIX® this is normally found at:

  ```
  ~/maya
  ```

- For Windows® this is normally at:

  ```
  \My Documents\maya
  ```

  If you do not find the *maya* directory there then check your other drives. This assumes that you have already installed and launched Maya at least once.

2 Rename the folder

Make sure the Maya application is closed, then temporarily rename the existing *maya* folder to something else. For example:

```
old_maya_folder
```

3 Copy the Data

Copy the *MEL_Fundamentals_DATA* folder from the CD to the same location that the *old_maya_folder* resides (do not put inside the folder - put at the same level). For example:

- For IRIX:

  ```
  ~/MEL_Fundamentals_DATA
  ```

- For Windows:

  ```
  \My Documents\MEL_Fundamentals_DATA
  ```

4 Rename the folder

- Rename `MEL_Fundamentals_DATA` to `maya`.

5 Launch Maya

Maya will now read all the preferences, projects, etc. from this folder. Once Maya is running, you should see the custom shelves used in this book.

If you want to go back to your original setup, exit Maya, reverse the folder names, and restart Maya. Then you will have all of your original shelves, hotkeys, marking menus, and other prefs back.

The process above lets you switch between the MEL Fundamentals setup and your own configuration. If you want to, you could merge the MEL data into your own *maya* folder so you don't have to keep switching. However, the process outlined above should get you going and is the recommended procedure to ensure that everything is in the correct location.

6 Set Your Project

Once you've launched Maya with the MEL Fundamentals data in place, set your project as follows:

File → Project → Set → \maya\projects\MF

Shelves/Prefs

There is one shelf tab for each chapter in the MEL Fundamentals book. These shelves contain most of the information from the book and can be used as a reference or can be copy/pasted for easier use as you go through the material. Not every entry in the shelf has a corresponding lesson or description in the MEL book, in some cases there is supplemental information that is used by the instructor to demonstrate a related concept.

Data-set list

Below is a breakdown of the subfolder contents. These pathnames assume that you have followed the installation procedure previously outlined.

\maya\5.0\scripts completed scripts for the book are stored here.

\maya\5.0\scripts\other contains scripts for demos and examples.

\maya\5.0\scripts\other\sample_UI extra UI script examples.

\maya\5.0\plugins plug-ins used by scenes.

\maya\5.0\prefs\icons contains image files which can be used in sample UI or on the shelves.

\maya\projects\MF\scenes contains all the needed scene files for the lessons.

\maya\projects\MF\scenes\appendix is where you will find the files from the appendix.

These scripts and data files are unsupported.

Help documentation

At any time during this book, you can refer to the on-line help documentation, usually installed by default with Maya. For a listing of general topics, click on **Help** → **Library...** or press the **F1** hotkey. To go directly to the MEL reference, click on **Help** → **MEL Command Reference**.

Customizing with MEL

Every time you use Maya, you are executing MEL commands. All of Maya's existing user interface is in some way derived from the use of MEL. This makes it very easy to customize your user interface using any or all of the following tools:

- **Shelf buttons** - The shelf is a repository for tools and commands that you use on a regular basis. You can add shelf tabs for different workflows. You can easily add MEL commands to the shelf for single click access.

- **Hotkeys** - Hotkeys are single key strokes that give you immediate access to tools and commands in Maya. An example of a hotkey would be the **s** key, which evokes the `setKeyframe` command. You can set up hotkeys to have quick access to specific MEL commands.

- **Marking menus** - Marking menus are radial menus that can be accessed either from the Hotbox or from a hotkey. You can assign MEL commands to the different parts of a marking menu.

In this lesson, you will learn how to use MEL to easily customize Maya to enhance your day-to-day workflows. Customizing Maya allows you to set up these workflow enhancements to streamline your productivity.

In this lesson, you will learn the following:

- How to create a macro
- How to create shelf buttons using the user interface
- How to create shelf buttons using MEL commands
- How to create hotkeys using MEL commands
- How to assign MEL commands to a marking menu

Script Editor

The Script Editor lets you execute and capture MEL scripts at any time. To display the Script Editor, select **Window** → **General Editors** → **Script Editor**.

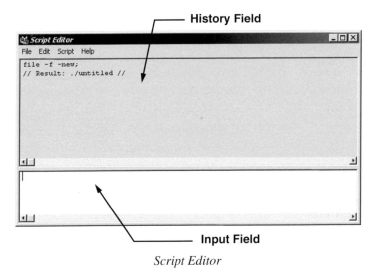

Script Editor

Use the bottom *Input* section of the Script Editor to enter commands. The top *History* section of the Script Editor displays executed MEL commands and their corresponding results, warnings, or errors.

Tip: Hold down **Ctrl** and use the mouse wheel to increase or decrease the size of the text for each field.

The History field

The upper part of the Script Editor is the *history* section. This section displays executed MEL commands and any feedback such as results, warnings, or errors returned by the system.

While you cannot input data in this section, you can highlight strings of commands and then click-drag this highlighted text to the lower input field or to a shelf.

The Input field

The lower part of the Script Editor is the *input* section. This field is like your scratchpad where you can write simple scripts before executing them. Listed below are a few of the things you can do with the input section:

- You can type or paste MEL commands for review.

- You can use the **Enter** key on the alphanumeric keyboard to start a new line within the input field without executing the script.

- You can use the **Enter** key on the numeric keypad when you want to execute the MEL script.

  If the MEL script executes without error, then the MEL script is removed from the input section and placed in the history section. If an error occurs, the MEL script is not removed from the input section and an error message is displayed in the history section.

- You can execute all or just a portion of the MEL script in the input section by highlighting the commands that you want to execute and then pressing the **Enter** key on the numeric keypad. Only the highlighted MEL script will be executed and all of the script will remain in the input section for further editing.

Tip: You can enter as many MEL commands as you want in the Script Editor, but each MEL command must terminate with a semicolon (;).

Macros

A macro is typically a combination of Maya commands combined to complete multiple functions in one step. A macro is created by a user to help reduce the number of commands they are executing to complete a task. Macros generally require no scripting and all of the commands in a macro can be grabbed from existing commands. You simply have to cut and paste them to a hotkey, shelf, or marking menu.

SHELF BUTTONS

Shelf buttons are another quick and easy way to customize your Maya environment. The shelves are displayed when the **Shelf** checkbox in the **Display → UI Elements** menu is checked. Contents of a shelf consist of buttons that have an associated MEL script. The following is an image of Maya's shelf:

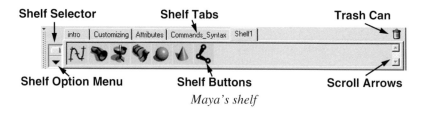

Maya's shelf

The shelves are laid out so that almost all of the shelf tabs are visible at once. Each tab represents a separate shelf. When you **LMB** (left mouse button) click on a tab, the contents of that shelf are displayed directly beneath the tabs. Shelf buttons comprise the contents of shelves.

The shelf selector is another way to select the current shelf. You can hide the tabs in the shelf option menu to gain some valuable work space and use the selector instead.

Shelf buttons are useful for easily executing a MEL command. Anything from a simple MEL command to an extremely complicated MEL script can be executed when you click on a shelf button. When you **LMB** click on a shelf button its associated MEL script is executed.

Shelf buttons can be reorganized or removed. To move a shelf button just **MMB** (middle mouse button) drag it to the desired position or tab, and it will move where you dropped it. More precise reordering can be done in the Shelves Editor. To insert a shelf button, drag the buttons one at a time to the desired location.

At the upper right hand portion of the shelves is a trash can symbol. This is used to remove shelf buttons. To remove a shelf button, just **MMB** drag it to the trash can symbol.

Tip: If there are too many shelf buttons to be displayed all at once, they will wrap around below the other buttons. They can be accessed by scrolling to them, using the arrow buttons at the right most part of the shelf.

Saving shelves

The shelves are saved in the **/maya/5.0/prefs/ shelves** directory.

Each shelf is saved in a seperate MEL file.

It is a good idea to backup these files. They can also be moved to other systems so you can have your own custom hotkeys on a different system.

Adding a shelf button that executes a menu item

Often it is convenient to have a shelf button execute one of Maya's menu items. In the following example you will add a shelf button to execute the **Create Emitter** menu item.

1   Create a new shelf: myShelf

- Select **Window → Settings/Preferences → Shelves...** to display the Shelf Editor.

- Under the **Shelves** tab, press the **New Shelf** button.

- Rename it *myShelf*, then press **Enter**.

- Press the **Save All Shelves** button.

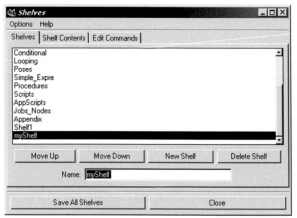

The Shelf Editor

Note: We will cover more of the Shelf Editor later in this chapter.

---

2 Display the myShelf shelf

- If your shelves are not visible, check the **Shelf** checkbox in the **Display → UI Elements** menu.

- Select the *myShelf* tab.

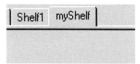

The myShelf tab

3 Add the shelf button for the Create Emitter menu item

- Press the **F4** key to go to the Dynamics menu set.

- Press the **Shift** and **Ctrl** keys, then with your **LMB**, select the **Particles → Create Emitter**.

  This menu item is now added to *myShelf*. Pressing the shelf button now invokes the same command as selecting the menu item from the menus.

New button on shelf

You can add any menu item that you want to a shelf by using the above method. You can even add a shelf button for a checkbox or tool setting menu selection. For example, you could create a shelf button for the **Display → UI Elements → Channel Box** or **Fields → Turbulence - ❏**. This would always take you to the option window of this menu choice.

Adding a shelf button that executes a MEL script

Besides adding shelf buttons that execute a menu selection, you can add shelf buttons that execute a MEL script.

In the example below, you will create two shelf buttons that, when executed, switch between a high resolution and low resolution version of a scene.

1 Open an existing scene file

- Select **File → Open Scene.**

- In the file browser, select *01.TrainHighLow.ma.*

2 Open the Script Editor and clear the history

- Select **Window → General Editors → Script Editor** to show the Script Editor.

- Select **Edit → Clear History** to empty whatever is in the history section of the Script Editor.

3 Select and hide the items not needed to animate

- Select **Window → Outliner.**

- Press the **Ctrl** button and go through the *Train* group to select the items to be hidden.

  When animating the train's major movements you would only need to see the *Cabin, Belly, Wheels, CabinBase* and *Engine* nodes. Everything else can be hidden.

- Type `hide` then press **Enter** on the numeric keypad.

4 Highlight and drag the command to the shelf

- With the **LMB**, highlight all the commands created in the history section of the Script Editor.

- Click and drag the highlighted MEL commands to anywhere in the *myShelf* button area.

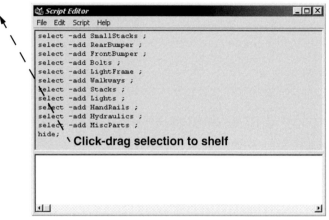

Dragging to shelf from Script Editor

The shelf button that you create will be added to the end of the buttons in *myShelf*. This button is now a macro that can optimize this scene for animation.

Note: By default, the button will have a MEL icon. You will see how to modify shelf buttons later in this chapter.

New button on shelf

To view the MEL script that is executed when you click on a certain shelf button, just **MMB** drag the shelf button to the bottom of the Script Editor.

5 Display the Hidden Geometry

- Select **Display → Show → Show Last Hidden**.

6 Highlight and drag the command to the shelf

- With the **LMB**, highlight the showHidden command line created in the history section of the Script Editor.
- Click and drag the highlighted command to the shelf.

This button is now a macro that can show what was last hidden.

Try out the buttons to see how they work. Later on you will learn a way to make these buttons into one button.

Tip: When highlighting items in the Script Editor you can save time by double clicking to highlight a single word or triple clicking to highlight an entire line. You can also use the **Ctrl + A** hotkey to select all the text.

A shelf button that executes several MEL commands

The previous exercise consisted of one line commands that let you execute functions in Maya. The following exercise is another simple example of creating a macro and making it into a shelf button by capturing commands. The difference is that this time, you will combine several commands in a single button.

In this exercise, you will create a shelf button that adds default lighting to any scene.

1 Start a new scene

- Select **File** → **New Scene**.

2 Open the Script Editor and clear the history section

- Select **Window** → **General Editors** → **Script Editor** to show the Script Editor.

- In the Script Editor select **Edit** → **Clear History** to empty the upper portion window.

3 Create a directional light

- Select **Create** → **Lights** → **Directional Light**.

- Name the light *frontLight*.

- **Rotate** the light to an appropriate direction facing away from the default camera direction.

4 Capture the commands

- In the history section of the Script Editor, use your **LMB** to highlight the commands for creating and rotating the light.

```
defaultDirectionalLight(1, 1,1,1, "0", 0,0,0);

rename "directionalLight1" "frontLight";

// Result: frontLight //
```

```
rotate -r -os -105.62 48.30 -72.77;
```

- Paste the highlighted commands by dragging them into the input section of the Script Editor.

5 Create a second directional light

- Select **Create** → **Lights** → **Directional Light**.

- Name the light *backLight*.

- **Rotate** the light to an appropriate direction facing towards the default camera position.

6 Capture the commands

- In the history section of the Script Editor, use your **LMB** to highlight the commands for creating and rotating the light.

```
defaultDirectionalLight(1, 1,1,1, "0", 0,0,0);

rename "directionalLight1" "backLight";

// Result: backLight //

rotate -r -os -83.2 -47.45 88;
```

- Drag and paste the highlighted commands at the end of the text in the input section of the Script Editor.

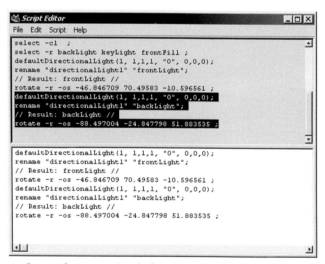

Output from creating lights shown in the Script Editor

7 Create a shelf button for your default lighting

- In the input section of the Script Editor, highlight all the commands.

- Drag the commands to the shelf.

  Maya will ignore any comment line starting with //. You can delete the result lines before dragging it to a shelf, with no harm to your macro.

Tip: If you have multiple move commands for one light you can combine them into one by copying the rotate values of X, Y and Z from the Channel Box and pasting them into the move command accordingly.

Exercise: Add more objects to your shelf

Practice creating and deleting some of your own custom shelf buttons. Buttons you may find useful are **Hide All**, **Show All**, creating other lighting schemes, or custom geometric primitives.

Echoing commands

In the previous exercises, you learned that when you execute an action using Maya's user interface the corresponding MEL commands that accomplish this same action are usually echoed to the history section of the Script Editor.

A good way to get familiar with different MEL commands is to use the user interface and look in the Script Editor to see what commands were used.

Sometimes, a user interface action does not automatically echo the corresponding commands in the Script Editor. In these cases, you will have to set up the Script Editor to echo all commands. To turn this option on, select **Script → Echo All Commands** from the Script Editor menu.

With *Echo All Commands* on, the MEL commands for almost any action executed by you or Maya are displayed in the history section of the Script Editor.

There is not always a one-to-one correspondence between what you think you have done and what MEL commands are echoed to the Script Editor. For example, with nothing selected, if you select **Windows → Attribute Editor...** to open the Attribute Editor, the following MEL commands might appear in the Script Editor (if *Echo All Commands* is on):

```
AttributeEditor;

openAEWindow;
```

However, either MEL command will bring up the Attribute Editor. Also, there are no corresponding MEL commands echoed to the Script Editor for some actions. For example, when you close the Attribute Editor, nothing is echoed in the history section of the Script Editor whether *Echo All Commands* is on or off.

Tip: To have hints on what these command are, use the `whatIs` command followed by the intriguing command name. It will give you good information about what the command is and/or where its coming from.

Only use the *Echo All Commands* when you need it. The amount of information that gets printed after some commands will slow down the performance of Maya. To turn off *Echo All Commands*, select **Script → Echo All Commands** again from the Script Editor.

EDITING SHELF BUTTONS

This section explores how you can edit existing shelf buttons. You will learn how to change the icon, label, tooltips, and functionality of a shelf button.

Changing the icon and label of shelf button

In the following example, you will change the icon and label of the MEL shelf button you just created.

1 Open the Shelves Editor and select myShelf

- Select **Window → Settings/Preferences → Shelves...**.
- Click on the **Shelves** tab at the top of the Shelves Editor.
- Make sure *myShelf* is selected in the list box at the top of the **Shelves** tab.

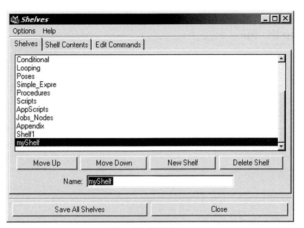

The Shelf Editor

In this tab there are buttons to create, delete, change order, and change name of shelves.

2 Select the MEL shelf button you just created

- Click on the **Shelf Contents** tab at the top of the Shelves Editor.

  Maya displays all the shelf buttons of the shelf that was selected in the **Shelves** tab.

- In the list box, click on the MEL script created in the last step, just below *Create Emitter*.

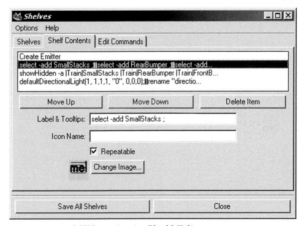

MEL script in Shelf Editor

In this tab there are buttons to delete, change the order and change the settings of shelf buttons.

3 Change the Label of the shelf button

- Remove the current **Label & Tooltips** description and then change it to the following:

```
Show Low resolution of TrainHighLow.
```

- Press the **Enter** key.

Tip: If **Help** → **Popup Help** is enabled, the button's tooltips is displayed when you move the mouse over the shelf button icons.

---

4 Change the Icon Name of the shelf button

- Type loRes in the button **Icon Name** field, then the **Enter** key.

If you look at the shelf button, you will see the first couple of letters of your icon name displayed over the shelf button.

Icon Name on shelf button

5 View the contents of the Edit commands tab

The **Edit Commands** tab is used for modifying the functionality of the shelf button that was selected in the **Shelf Contents** tab. Since a shelf button just executes MEL commands, you can edit the MEL commands associated with any shelf button.

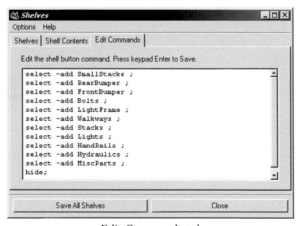

Edit Commands tab

Editing Icons

You can also create, modify, and use your own images as icons. If you place your images in **/maya/5.0/prefs/icons/** directory, you can use those images by browsing to that directory.

Images can be edited using any paint application.

Icons are normally .xpm format on IRIX and .bmp on Windows, but both are supported.

Note:	While changing the button's script or setting, if you change tabs, you may be prompted to save or discard changes.

6 Change the image of the shelf button icon

- Click on the **Change Image...** button in the **Shelf Contents** tab of the **Shelves** Editor.

- Select *userMenuIconAdd.xpm* (IRIX) or *userMenuIconAdd.bmp* (Windows) from the images listing.

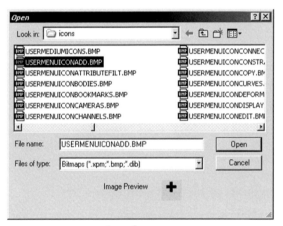

Icon browser

- Confirm your selection.

7 Save the changes you made to the shelves

- Click on the **Save All Shelves** button to save the shelf modifications, if desired.

  By default, Maya will save your shelves upon closing, but it will not be saved in case of an unwanted Maya ending (kill or crash). Always make sure to save them using one of the three following options:

- In the option menu in the shelf UI, select **Save All Shelves**.

- Under **Window** → **Settings/Preferences** → **Preferences...** click **Save**.

- Select **Save Preferences** under the **File** main menu.

HOTKEYS

One of the easiest ways to customize Maya is to create custom hotkeys. Hotkeys allow you to instantly access anything from a simple MEL command to an involved MEL script with a single keystroke. Although hotkeys can only execute MEL scripts, almost everything Maya does can be done using a MEL script.

Adding a hotkey to clear the current selection list

In this example, you will add a hotkey that will clear the current selection list. You will use the Hotkey Editor to do this. In this editor, you first create what is called a *command object*. This is a MEL script with an annotation label. You will create a hotkey associated with this command object that will execute the corresponding MEL script when it is invoked.

1 Open the Hotkeys Editor

- Select **Window** → **Settings/Preferences** → **Hotkeys...**

    The Hotkey Editor will appear.

The Hotkey Editor

2 Add a command for clearing the selection list

- Press **New**.

- Enter `clearSelection` in the **Name** field and also enter a **Description** like "`Clear selection list`".

  The name must start with a letter and no space or special characters are allowed.

- Set **Category** to **User**.

- Enter the following in the **Command** field:

  `select -clear;`

- Click **Accept**.

Note:　　When you created the `clearSelection` command, it was automatically selected.

3　Specify the Ctrl + Alt + d hotkey for the new command

- In the **Assign New Hotkey** section, check the **Ctrl** and **Alt** checkboxes and type **d** in the **Key** field.

- Click the **Query** button to determine if the hotkey is already assigned. If it is already assigned, you can pick a new hotkey in order to not overwrite the existing one.

  You can use the **List All...** button for a list of assigned hotkeys to determine which one you can use.

Saving hotkeys

The hotkey settings are saved in the **/maya/5.0/ prefs/** directory.

They are saved in two files: *userHotkeys.mel* and *userNamedCommands.mel*.

It is a good idea to backup these files. They can also be moved to other systems so you can have your own custom hotkeys on a different system.

Tip:　　Hotkeys are case-sensitive. To specify uppercase letters, enter an uppercase letter in the **Key** field. An uppercase letter requires the use of the **Shift** key.

You can also specify whether the command is executed upon the press or release of the hotkey for creating a temporary UI, such as a marking menu.

4　Accept the selected key

- Click the **Assign** button to create the hotkey.

  When you click this button, the hotkey specified in the **Key** field is applied to the command object that is selected in the upper right portion of the Hotkey Editor. Note that the hotkey is NOT written to the preference file until you click on the **Save** button, close Maya, or select **File → Save Preference**.

5　Save the hotkey as a preference

- Click on the **Save** button at the bottom of the Hotkey Editor then press the **Close** button.

This saves the changes you made so they will be present during the current and subsequent Maya sessions.

6 Practice using this hotkey

- Create some objects and select any combination of them.

- Type the **Ctrl + Alt + d** hotkey that you just created to remove all the selected objects from the selection list.

  The hotkey you created was mapped to a command object annotation which corresponds to the MEL script you entered. Now, whenever you press this hotkey, the MEL script clearSelection will be executed.

  You can also have a hotkey execute any menu item that you want. To do this just select the corresponding category and command object in the upper portion of the Hotkey Editor, specify a hotkey, and click the **Assign** and **Save** buttons.

MARKING MENUS™

Marking menus are menus that pop up at the current mouse position when a mouse button is pressed down (usually in combination with a hotkey). Its menu items can be selected by dragging the mouse cursor in a radial direction and releasing the mouse button. The possible radial directions are north, south, east, west, and diagonals (north-east, north-west, south-east, south-west). An example of a marking menu is shown below:

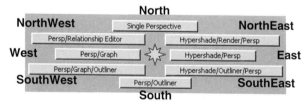

A marking menu

Marking menus give you nearly the speed of hotkeys while being as visual as regular pull-down menus. Additionally, marking menus can be built on top of each other in any hierarchical organization that you choose by using submenus. This provides you with a great depth of organized menu items with a minimum of mouse actions.

Accessing marking menus

There are two ways that a marking menu can be accessed. One way is by using a **hotkey** and the other is by using the **Hotbox**. To display the

Hotbox, press and hold down the **Space bar** with the Maya workspace enabled. Maya displays the Hotbox at the location of the mouse cursor. The Hotbox is illustrated below:

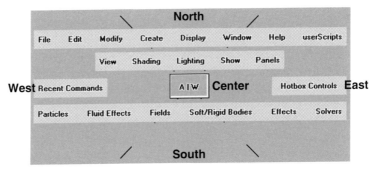

The Hotbox

Note: By pressing the space bar quickly without holding it down, the view will toggle from the four panel to a single panel view.

The Hotbox gives you quick access to all menus found in the main window of Maya as well as its workspace. The Hotbox has five zones: North (up), South (down), East (right), West (left), and Center. They are defined by diagonal lines. Each zone outside of a menu can contain marking menus.

For example, to display the marking menu associated with the North zone of the Hotbox, bring up the Hotbox by holding down the space bar over the Maya workspace, move the mouse up past the top Hotbox menus, and press any mouse button. You should see a marking menu displayed at the current mouse position.

To access a marking menu using a hotkey, just hold down the hotkey over the Maya workspace and click down the mouse button that brings up the marking menu. For example, to access the marking menu that changes the current menu set, hold down the **h** key over the Maya workspace and click down the **LMB**.

Tip: When you release the mouse button with the mouse cursor over the center of the marking menu, the marking menu disappears without selecting one of its menu selections.

Assigning a MEL script to a marking menu item

Assigning a MEL script to a marking menu item is conceptually no different than assigning a MEL script to a hotkey. In the following example, you will create a new marking menu that can be accessed by clicking down on the **LMB** while, at the same time, holding down the **m** hotkey.

First, however, you will create a new marking menu and assign a MEL script to one of its selection items.

1 Create a new marking menu called Mine

- Select **Window** → **Settings/Preferences** → **Marking Menus...** to bring up the Marking Menus Editor.

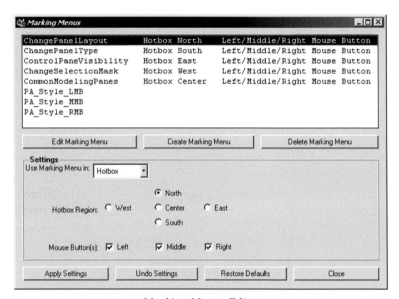

Marking Menus Editor

Tip: If necessary, click and drag the lower right corner of the window to enlarge the editor.

The list box at the top of the Marking Menus dialog displays the name of the existing marking menus and how they are accessed. For example, the first marking menu displayed in the text box is named *ChangePanelLayout* and is accessed by clicking on either the left, middle, or right mouse button when the mouse cursor is over the North part of the Hotbox. This access setting can be changed by modifying the specifications in the Settings section.

- Click on the **Create Marking Menu** button to create a new marking menu.

At the top of the Create Marking Menu dialog that appears, there are place holders for the marking menu radial selection items.

- In the **Menu Name** text box, type *Mine* followed by the **Enter** key.

The name must start with a letter and must not contain space or special characters.

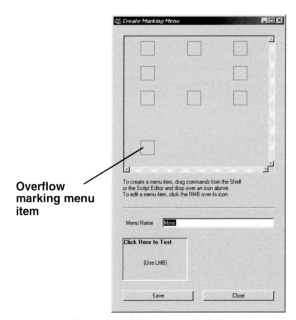

Create marking menu window

Tip: The marking menu selection item to the lower left of the radial selection items represents the overflow marking menu item. You can add more than one overflow marking menu item. These overflow marking menu items appear beneath the radial marking menu items.

---

2 Capture commands in the Script Editor for your marking menu

- Select **Window** → **General Editors** → **Script Editor** to show the Script Editor.

- Select a menu command using the user interface so that its commands appear in the Script Editor. Make sure to *Echo All Commands* if the command you are seeking does not appear in the Script Editor.

  Some example commands used here are:

  ```
  HideAll;
  ShowAll;
  ```

3 Add the script to the marking menu

- With your **LMB**, highlight the MEL command in the Script Editor.

- With your **MMB**, drag the highlighted MEL script to the Northwest (upper left) marking menu selection item in the **Create Marking Menu** window.

  After you do this, a MEL icon will appear in the Northwest marking menu selection position in the **Create Marking Menu** dialog.

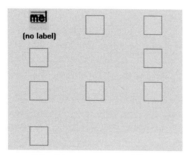

Marking menu positions

4 Label the marking menu selection item

- With the **RMB**, click on the label of the Northwest marking menu you just created and select **Edit Menu Item** in the menu that pops up.

  In this **RMB** pop up menu there are also selection items to delete or make it a popup submenu. A popup submenu is a new marking menu that appears at the mouse cursor position when it is selected.

  When you select this marking menu item, a new marking menu appears that can contain any other marking menu selection items that you choose, including other popup submenus. This allows you to build a powerful hierarchy of marking menus.

Shelf button in Marking Menu

As indicated in the middle of the **Create Marking Menu** window, you can also drag a shelf button to a marking menu selection item. To create a menu item, drag commands from the Shelf or the Script Editor and drop over an icon above. To edit a menu item, click the **RMB** over its icon.

- Type *Hide All* in the **Label** field of the Edit North West window that pops up.

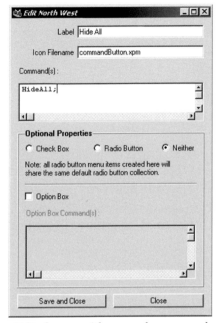

Edited name with a sample command

Note: In this dialog, you can modify the marking menu selection item. You can change the MEL script that is executed when the marking menu selection item is selected. You can also make the marking menu selection item a check box or radio button, however, these two options do not provide any additional functionality—they are just for looks.

On the other hand, an option box, (❒), can be added to the right hand side of the marking menu selection item to execute any other MEL script that you desire. You can add an option box by checking the **Option Box** checkbox and **MMB** dragging a shelf button or MEL script from the Script Editor to the **Option Box Commands(s)** text box.

- Click on the **Save and Close** button in the Edit North West window.

If you just close this dialog, none of the changes made in it would be applied.

5 Test and save the Mine marking menu

- To test the *Mine* marking menu, click and hold with the **LMB** in the lower left box of the **Create Marking Menu** window that is labeled **Click Here to Test (Use LMB)**.

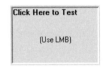

Marking Menu test area

- Click on **Save,** followed by the **Close** button in the **Create Marking Menu** dialog.

  If you close this dialog without saving, none of the changes made in it would be applied.

- Notice that in the **Marking Menus** window, the *Mine* marking menu is now displayed and selected.

6 Make the new marking menu available in the Hotkey Editor

- With *Mine* menu selected, in the **Settings** section, select **Hotkey Editor** in the **Use Marking Menu in** setting.

  Notice that when you select the **Hotkey Editor** in **Use Marking Menu in**, the following message appears in the Settings section of the dialog:

  The Marking Menu will be available for editing in the Hotkey Editor.

  This means that you must specify a hotkey in the Hotkey Editor for accessing the marking menu.

Tip: There are two other selections for the **Use Marking Menu in** setting. One is **Hotbox**, which indicates that the marking menu can be accessed in the Hotbox. The other is **(not set)**, which indicates that the marking menu can not be accessed by using either a hotkey or the Hotbox.

- Click on the **Apply Settings** button in the **Marking Menus** window.
- Click on the **Close** button in the **Marking Menus** window.

Specifying a hotkey for accessing a marking menu

Now that you have created the marking menu, you need to be able to access it. In the following example, you will make an **m** hotkey that will be used to access your *Mine* marking menu.

Testing marking menus

When you select a marking menu selection item in test mode, Maya actually executes that menu selection item.

---

1 **Open the Hotkeys Editor**

- Select **Window** → **Settings/Preferences** → **Hotkeys...**

2 **Specify the m-Press hotkey for Mine**

- Locate the **User Marking Menus** entry at the bottom of the **Categories** field of the Hotkey Editor.

- Select **Mine_Press** in the **Commands** field just to the right of the **Categories**.

- Type **m** in the **Key** field of the **Assign New Hotkey** section.

- Click on the **Press** radio button in the **Assign New Hotkey** section.

- Click **Assign.**

  You may be prompted to confirm the override with the new hotkey assignment. If so, click on the **Assign** button.

3 **Automatically specify the m-Release hotkey for Mine**

- The Hotkey Editor will ask if you want the **Mine_Release** to be also assigned to the **m-Release** hotkey. Click on **Yes**.

Note: You must specify the press and release marking menu command objects to use the same hotkey. If you don't, then your marking menu might not disappear after you are finished using it. If you encounter this problem, you can temporarily fix it by executing the release commands associated with your marking menu hotkey in the Script Editor.

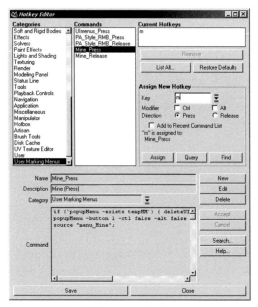

Hotkey Editor press/release setup

4 Save these hotkey preferences

- Click **Save** then **Close** at the bottom of the Hotkey Editor.

5 Practice accessing the Mine marking menu

- Create several primitive objects.

- Click in the Maya workspace to enable it, then press the **m** key and click and hold the **LMB**.

  The *Mine* marking menu should appear at the position of the mouse cursor.

- Drag the mouse cursor in the upper right direction and select the **Hide All** Northwest marking menu selection item.

- View the printed results in the top portion of the Script Editor with *Echo All Commands* on.

Note: Marking menus used in the Hotkey Editor can only be accessed by using the **LMB** in combination with the hotkey.

Creating Custom Work Environments

In all the previous examples, you were able to simply see the commands that you executed in the user interface in the Script Editor. In the following lesson, you will set up custom work environments for animating, modeling and rendering, using *Echo All Commands* to see the commands used to create these interfaces.

In this example, you will build a macro as a marking menu item for quickly setting up a customized modeling interface layout.

1 Open the Script Editor and turn on Echo All Commands

- Select **Window** → **General Editors** → **Script Editor** to show the Script Editor.

- Select **Edit** → **Clear History** in the Script Editor to empty whatever is in the history section.

- Select **Edit** → **Echo All Commands** in the Script Editor to turn on the verbose mode of Maya.

2 Change the Interface to your typical modeling environment

- Select **Display** → **UI Elements** → **Hide UI Elements.**

- Capture the command from the history section of the Script Editor and copy it to the input section.

  ```
  setAllMainWindowComponentsVisible 0;
  ```

  Selecting **Hide UI Elements** sets the interface so that you can add only those user interface elements that you want.

- Select the following components from the **Display** → **UI Elements** menu.

  Status Line

  Shelf

  Command Line

  Channel Box / Layer Editor

  You may prefer to have different setup so feel free to use the components that work best for your workflow.

- Capture the commands to reproduce these steps.

  ```
  ToggleStatusLine;
  ToggleShelf;
  ToggleCommandLine;
  ToggleChannelsLayers;
  ```

3 Set a Pane Layout

- Select **Window** → **Saved Layouts** → **Persp/Outliner.**

- Capture the command from the Script Editor.

```
setNamedPanelLayout "Persp/Outliner";
```

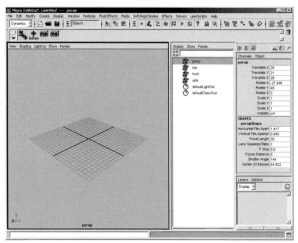

A possible user interface layout

4 Add the script to a marking menu

- Select **Windows** → **Settings/Preferences** → **Marking Menus...**

- Create a marking menu like you did in the previous lesson for your modeling interface.

Selected script commands

Exercise: Create other layouts for the marking menu

Now create an animation and rendering interface and add them to the same marking menu. Remember to **Hide UI Elements** first to clear the interface and to capture all of the commands to create each environment.

Saving Marking Menus

The marking menu files are saved in the **/maya/5.0/prefs/ markingMenus** directory.

Each marking menu is saved as a seperate MEL file. However, the settings for all your marking menus are located in *userPrefs.mel*.

It is a good idea to back up your marking menu files and the *userSetup.mel* file in case something happens to your system. They can also be copied to other systems so you can have your own custom preferences when using Maya.

Saving preferences using userSetup.mel

You can use the user interface to save many Maya user preferences. To retain preferences that are not saved in the user interface, create a `userSetup.mel` file in your script path. Whenever you launch Maya, the MEL commands in it are executed.

An example command used in the `userSetup.mel` file is the following:

```
alias djs jointDisplayScale;
```

This creates an alias, *djs*, that lets you set the joint size without using the **Joint Size** menu or typing `jointDisplayScale`. You can enter the *djs* alias with a joint size in the Command Line or Script Editor:

```
djs 1.5;
```

The joint size is set to 1.5.

Note: By default, the scene is cleared after the commands in the `userSetup.mel` file are executed. Therefore, any scene elements created using the `userSetup.mel` file will have been removed when Maya comes up.

Key objectives covered

In this lesson, you have learned how to use MEL to customize Maya so that you can be very efficient and free in your workflow. You have learned to customize the following items in Maya.

- Shelf buttons

- Hotkeys

- Marking menus

Exercises

1 Shelf buttons

- Practice setting up some shelf buttons using the appropriate labels. For example, create a layouts shelf that will arrange your window layouts with your most commonly used UI setups.

2 Hotkeys

- Practice creating hotkeys by opening the Script Editor and capturing commands from the upper panel and putting them into hotkeys.

3 Marking menus

- Create several marking menus with multiple MEL commands.

2 Attributes

Maya's system architecture uses a procedural paradigm that lets you integrate traditional keyframe animation, inverse kinematics, dynamics, and scripting on top of a node-based architecture that is called the **Dependency graph**. If you wanted to reduce this graph to its bare essentials, you could describe it as *nodes with attributes that are connected*. This node-based architecture gives Maya its flexible procedural qualities.

When working with MEL, you will often write scripts that work with nodes and attributes. This lesson teaches you how attribute information is stored in Maya and how to access and modify that information.

In this lesson, you will learn the following:

- How to recognize an attribute

- How to view and edit attributes using the following tools:

    Channel Box
    Attribute Editor

- How to work with attribute related MEL commands such as:

    listAttr
    getAttr
    setAttr
    aliasAttr

- How to connect attributes using the Connection Editor

- How to connect attributes using the following commands:

    connectAttr
    disconnectAttr

- Adding and deleting attributes with the Attribute Editor using:

```
addAttr
deleteAttr
```

- Listing nodes and obtaining node information with:

```
listConnections
listRelatives
ls
```

What is an attribute?

Every element in Maya, whether it is a curve, surface, deformer, light, texture, expression, modeling operation, or animation curve, is described by either a single node or a series of connected nodes.

Each node is defined by a series of attributes that relate to what the node is designed to accomplish. In the case of a transform node, *Translate X* is an attribute. In the case of a material node, *Color R* is an attribute. It is possible for you to assign values to the attributes to change the effect of the node. Later in this lesson, you will learn how to work with attributes using the user interface elements such as the Attribute Editor and the Channel Box.

One important feature in Maya is that you can animate virtually every attribute on any node. This helps give Maya its animation power. You should also note that attributes are also referred to as *channels*.

Connecting attributes

Nodes and attributes cannot live in isolation. A finished animation results when you begin making connections between attributes on different nodes. These connections are also known as dependencies. You will learn more about these connections at the end of this lesson.

Attribute types

There are three types of attributes: *static, dynamic,* and *custom*.

Static attributes always exist. A *nurbSphere* will always be created with certain attributes which cannot be removed such as *translate, rotate, scale,* and *visibility*.

Dynamic attributes are added to certain objects. A *particleShape* node can have dynamic attributes added such as *lifespan, color,* and *opacity*. Dynamic attributes can be added and removed from a node.

Custom attributes are attributes added to an object for additional control. If you had a character setup, you might put a custom attribute on the *wrist* node called *fingerCurl*. This custom attribute would control the amount the fingers curl. Custom attributes can be added and removed from a node.

Why do I want to know about attributes?

Almost all of the data in a scene is stored in the attributes of the scene objects. In other words, the scene is defined by the attributes of the objects in it.

To create objects and modify them, you need to change attributes. To animate your scene, you need to connect the attributes to animation curve nodes.

Viewing and modifying attribute values

You will learn how to set attributes and change their values. You can view or change the value of an attribute by using any of the following:

- Channel Box

- Attribute Editor

- The getAttr and setAttr commands

- The aliasAttr command

- The connectAttr and disconnectAttr command

The MEL commands used to view or change the values of an attribute are the getAttr and setAttr commands, respectively.

CHANNEL BOX

The Channel Box is useful for gaining quick access to the *keyable* attributes of an object. Keyable attributes are attributes that can be keyframed when you use **Set key**, but it does not mean you cannot key them. You can use the Channel Box for both viewing the attribute values and modifying them.

Accessing attributes in the Channel Box

To use the Channel Box, it must be visible and an object needs to be selected. You can have multiple objects selected and in these cases, any attributes that are shared amongst the selected nodes will all be edited together. You will know that you have multiple objects selected when the object name is followed by three dots (e.g.: *nurbsPlane1...*)

1 Display the Channel Box

- **Select** an object.

- If the Channel Box is hidden, select **Display** → **UI Elements** → **Channel Box / Layer Editor**.

  The Channel Box appears on the right side of the Maya window.

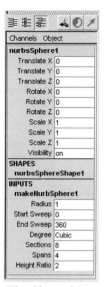

The Channel Box

The Channel Box displays the keyable attributes (and their values) of the selected object(s).

To modify the object attributes displayed in the Channel Box, click with **LMB** in the corresponding text box, replace the value in it, then press the **Enter** key.

Some attributes cannot be modified. These attributes may be controlled by an expression, a connection, or they can be locked.

Tip: Another way to edit a value in the Channel Box is to **LMB** select the attribute, then **MMB** click and drag in the modeling view to activate a *virtual* slider.

Long, short, or nice names in the Channel Box

All attributes have a name associated with them. That name can be long or abbreviated (short). You can specify which name you wish to appear in the Channel Box as the following example illustrates.

1 Open the Channel Names menu

- At the top of the Channel Box, select **Channels** → **Channel Names**.
- Select a naming option.

Long lists the attributes by their long name.

translateX, startSweep

Short lists the attributes by their short name.

tx, ssw

Nice displays the long name with a few modifications. The first letter is capitalized, then a space is inserted between characters where a lowercase letter is followed by an uppercase one.

Translate X, Start Sweep

ATTRIBUTE EDITOR

You can also modify the attributes of an object using the Attribute Editor. The Attribute Editor contains more attributes than the Channel Box since it contains both keyable and non-keyable attributes.

1 Select an object in the modeling view

- Select or create an object, for example, a *nurbsPlane*.

- Select **Window → Attribute Editor**.

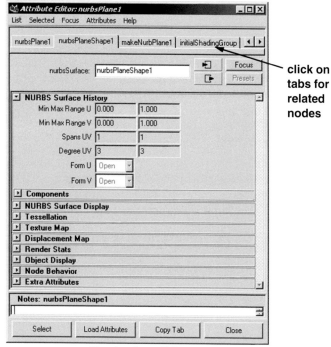

click on tabs for related nodes

The Attribute Editor

The tabs at the top of the Attribute Editor give you access to nodes related to the currently selected object. In each tab, attributes and their corresponding values are displayed for the node indicated by the label of the tab. These values are usually modifiable with some sort of text box or UI control, such as sliders, pull-down list, check box, etc.

Tip: To use virtual sliders in the Attribute Editor, hold down the **Ctrl** key and use the **LMB, MMB** or **RMB** in the value field. The rate at which the field values change depends on which button you use.

Shape nodes

When you create a sphere, by default, a *nurbsSurface* shape node parented to a transform node is created. If you bring up the Attribute Editor when just the sphere transform node is selected, it comes up with tabs for the transform node of the object, the *nurbsSurfaceShape* node, the *makeNurbsSurface* shape history node, and the shader node that is applied to the *nurbsSurfaceShape* node.

Notice that the shape object tab is displayed by default rather than the transform object even though the transform is what you selected. This is because you will generally want to access the attributes of the shape instead of its generic transform.

The shape node usually contains the attributes specific to the object that you create. For example, a particle shape node will have attributes for velocity, acceleration and render type. A *nurbsSurface* shape node will have attributes for spans, divisions, and tessellation.

Transform nodes

A transform node is almost always created as a parent for almost any object that you create. This transform node contains generic attributes that apply to almost all objects. These attributes include translate, rotate, scale, shear, pivot, display, bounding box, and other basic information.

USING MEL TO ACCESS ATTRIBUTES

Another way to get attribute information is to use MEL commands.

The syntax for referring to the attributes of a node is:

```
nodeName.attributeName
```

The name of the node and the attribute are written together, separated by a period. For example, the *translateX* attribute of *nurbsSphere1* would be written like

    nurbsSphere1.translateX *(Long name)*

    or

    nurbsSphere1.tx *(Short name)*

Naming abbreviations

You can use the short names for almost all of the attributes in Maya. This can make MEL writing a little quicker and easier to read.

Example:

    ball.tx (translateX)

    ball.sz (scaleZ)

These are some commonly used short names:

Long Name	Abrev.
translateX	tx
translateY	ty
translateZ	tz
rotateX	rx
rotateY	ry
rotateZ	rz
scaleX	sx
scaleY	sy
scale	sz
visibility	v

Listing object attributes

To find out what attributes exist for an object, use the listAttr command.

Syntax

    listAttr [flags] [objects]

Common listAttr flags

-c -connectable

-k -keyable

-l -locked

-u -unlocked

-sn -shortNames

-v -visible

-ud -userDefined

Example

```
listAttr -keyable nurbsSphere
```

If the object is active then you only have to enter the following:

```
listAttr -keyable
```

Note: To view the flags available for a command, type `help commandName` in the Script Editor. For example: `help listAttr`. The other source for reference is the on-line help documents, accessed from the Help menu either from the main window or the Script Editor.

The [ ] characters above means optional arguments for the command.

---

getattr command

The `getAttr` command gives you quick access to data even if the attribute is not keyable. This may be preferred over the Channel Box which displays only the keyable attributes of an object and over the Attribute Editor where attributes may be hidden under tabs or partitions.

Common getAttr flags

-k -keyable

-l -lock

-s -size

-t -time

-typ -type

Syntax

```
getAttr [flags] object.attribute
```

Example

```
getAttr nurbsSphere1.translateX
getAttr nurbsSphere1.tx
```

Displaying attributes with the getattr command

You can use a simple primitive sphere to show how to list and get information from an attribute.

1 Create a sphere in the Script Editor

- Select **Window → General Editors → Script Editor**.
- Enter the following command to create a sphere:

    ```
    sphere;
    ```

- Press **Enter** on the numeric keypad.

2 View what attributes are keyable

- Enter the following command:

    ```
    listAttr -keyable;
    ```

3 Get the value of the sphere's Translate X Attribute

- Enter the following command:

```
getAttr nurbsSphere1.translateX;
```

setattr **command**

The setAttr command provides a quick way to set the value of an attribute.

Syntax

```
setAttr [flags] object.attribute [value]
```

Example

```
setAttr nurbsSphere1.translateX 15
```

1 Enter the setattr command in the Script Editor

- Open the Script Editor.
- **LMB** click in the lower portion of the Script Editor.
- Enter the command as follows:

```
setAttr nurbsSphere1.translateX 3;
```

- Press the **Enter** key to execute the command.

Common setAttr flags
-e -edit
-q -query
-k -keyable
-l -lock
-typ -type

Adding an alias to an attribute with aliasattr

You can also change the name of an attribute by adding an alias to it. This allows you to create custom names for each attribute or names that are more descriptive than *rotateX* or *scaleY*. For example, if you've created a model of a car and the translateX attribute of the car represents the forward movement of the car, you could add an alias to the translateX attribute and call it *forward*.

For this exercise, create a sphere and change the translateY attribute to the word *up*.

Syntax

```
aliasAttr [flags] [aliasName]
   [objectname.realAttribute]
```

Example

- To add an alias, type:

```
aliasAttr "up" nurbsSphere1.translateY;
```

In the channel box the translateY attribute is now called *up*.

- To remove the alias, use the -remove flag:

```
aliasAttr -remove nurbsSphere1.up;
```

Common aliasAttr flags
-q -query
-rm -remove

CONNECTING AND DISCONNECTING ATTRIBUTES

In order for nodes and attributes to participate in the dependency graph, they must be connected. You can either connect attributes using expressions, which places an extra node in-between the two connected nodes, or you can directly connect the attributes using either the Connection Editor or the `connectAttr` command. These let you establish a direct relationship between two attributes that evaluates very fast.

For example, if you wanted the *translateY* attribute value of a cone to always equal the *translateX* attribute value of a sphere you could connect these two attributes. You can only connect from one attribute to one or more other attributes. This means that one attribute controls the other attributes. The controlling attribute can be modified but the controlled attributes cannot since their value is derived from the controlling attribute.

Furthermore, you should not create a cycle of attribute connections, i.e. you should not connect attribute A to attribute B and then connect attribute B to attribute A. If you do create a cycle of attribute connections you may not be able to modify any of the attributes in the cycle.

Connection Editor

Connection Editor

The Connection Editor defaults to Auto-connect mode on (set under Options). This means that you would highlight the output attribute and highlight the input attribute to make a connection. To break a connection, simply toggle the input attribute off.

Provided Auto-connect mode is off, connections can be made with the **Make** button, at the bottom of the Connection Editor window. To break a connection, select the attributes and press the **Break** button.

The Connection Editor is used to connect attributes from one object to another. When two objects are selected and loaded into the Connection Editor you will be able to see all the available attributes for connecting. When you select an attribute on the left side of the Connection Editor which is the output side, then the attributes that you can't connect to are grayed out.

1 Create two primitive objects

- Create a primitive sphere and name it *ball*.
- Create a primitive cone and name it *spike*.

2 Load the two nodes in the Connection Editor

- Select **Window** → **General Editors** → **Connection Editor....**
- **Select** the *ball* node.
- In the Connection Editor, click the **Reload Left** button.

  The *ball* attributes appear in the **Output** attributes, which is the left column of the Connection Editor. These are the attributes you'll use to control the specified input attributes.

- **Select** the *spike* node.

- In the Connection Editor, click the **Reload Right** button.

  The attributes of the *spike* node are now in the **Input** attributes, the right column of the Connection Editor.

3 Connect the two nodes

- In the **Output** column, expand the *Translate* attribute item.

  The *Translate X, Translate Y,* and *Translate Z* attributes appear.

- Click on the *Translate X* attribute of the *ball*.

  In the **Input** column, the *Translate* attribute is grayed out. That is because you cannot connect attributes of incompatible types.

- Expand the *Translate* attribute item in the **Input** column.

  The *Translate X, Translate Y,* and *Translate Z* attributes appear.

- Click the *Translate Y* attribute of the *spike*.

  A connection is now made from the selected output to the selected input. Here, the *ball Translate X* attribute is connected to (and therefore controls) the *Translate Y* attribute of the *spike*. The text of the connected attributes should be italicized to show they are connected.

4 Test the results

- **Select** and **Move** the *ball* in **X** and see how the *spike* is automatically moved in **Y**.

  Notice that you cannot change the *spike Translate Y* manually because it has an input connection.

5 Disconnect the attributes

- In the Connection Editor, click on the *Translate X* attribute of the *ball*.

  The *Translate Y* attribute of the *spike* will be highlighted.

- Toggle off the *Translate Y* attribute of the *spike*.

  Make sure it is no longer italicized. The attributes are now disconnected.

Using MEL's `connectattr` and `disconnectattr`

You can also connect and disconnect attributes using MEL commands.

Syntax

```
connectAttr sourceAttribute destinationAttribute
```

Other helpful MEL attribute commands

The **attributeQuery** command can be used to check for the existence of an attribute first before an addAttr statement is invoked.

The command **listHistory** will show you what nodes are in the history list. If they are in the history list then there will be attributes connected between the nodes. This is useful for finding connections up stream or down stream of the active node.

The command **nodeType** can be used to determine what type of node is active.

This connection means if you change the value of the *sourceAttribute*, then the *destinationAttribute* value changes automatically.

Example

```
connectAttr sphere.translateX cone.translateY;
connectAttr sphere.tx cone.ty;
```

Syntax

```
disconnectAttr sourceAttribute destinationAttribute
```

This command breaks the connection between the *sourceAttribute* and the *destinationAttribute*.

Example

```
disconnectAttr sphere.translateX cone.translateY;
disconnectAttr nurbsSphere1.tx cone.ty;
```

Example: Spike and Ball

In this example, you will re-create the cone and sphere example explained above using only MEL. First, you will create a cone and a sphere and then connect the *translateY* value of the cone to the *translateX* value of the sphere.

1 Create a cone and a sphere using MEL

- Open a new scene.
- Enter the following commands:

```
cone -name "spike";
sphere -name "ball";
move 0 0 5;
```

2 Connect ball and spike using MEL

- Enter the following command:

```
connectAttr ball.translateX spike.translateY;
```

This command connects the **translateX** attribute of the *ball* node into the **translateY** attribute of *spike* node.

3 Test the results

- **Move** the *ball* along the X axis to see the effect on *spike*.

Notice that when *ball* object moves up the X axis, *spike* moves up the Y axis and vice versa. However, you cannot move *spike* in the Y direction directly because *spike*'s Y translate is being controlled by the translate X attribute of *ball*.

4 Disconnect the two nodes using MEL

- Enter the following command:

```
disconnectAttr ball.translateX spike.translateY;
```

  This command disconnects the two attributes. Now when you **Move** the *ball* node nothing happens to the *spike* node.

Maya FX Example: Working with an emitter

This example creates a particle emitter to emit in a direction that always points away from the origin no matter where the emitter is moved to. This would be useful for a comet or fireball. You can easily do this if you make the emission direction attributes equal to position attributes of the emitter.

1 Create a directional emitter with a spread of 0.3

- Go to the **Dynamics** menu set.

- Select **Particles → Create Emitter**.

- In the Channel Box, under *emitter1*, **LMB** select **Directional** in the **Emitter Type** pull-down list.

  When you **LMB** select the text field corresponding to the **Emitter Type**, a pull-down list will appear with several choices.

- Change also the **Spread** of *emitter1* to **0.3**.

2 Connect the emitter's translation to its direction

- Enter the following commands:

```
connectAttr emitter1.translateX emitter1.directionX;
connectAttr emitter1.translateY emitter1.directionY;
connectAttr emitter1.translateZ emitter1.directionZ;
```

  These commands connect the position attributes of the emitter to its direction attributes.

Tip: Double-click on a word or triple-click on a line and use copy/paste for faster typing. You may also use the attribute short names.

---

3 Move the emitter around and play the scene

Notice that the particles are always emitted in directions away from the origin. Try moving the emitter to the origin and see what happens.

You will notice that as you move the emitter in X, Y or Z, their values increase from 0. Since you connected these attributes to the emission direction of the particles, as you move the emitter further from origin, the emission direction is also increasing.

You might want to try and make additional connections between attributes. Possibilities include connecting attributes between attributes of the same object or making connections from one attribute to several other attributes, but not making connections from many attributes to only one attribute.

ADDING ATTRIBUTES

In Maya, you can also add your own attributes. These attributes can then be connected to other nodes to give you additional controls for your scene. Attributes can be added using either the user interface or with MEL commands. You can also remove attributes with the user interface or MEL commands but you can only remove those attributes that have been added on the object by the user.

Custom attributes

The main reason to add custom attributes to an object is to control the attributes of other objects. This can help with workflow since picking one object and setting keyframes on its attributes can be quicker than switching to different objects.

For example, you could create an empty transformation node and add attributes which would control the intensity of the lights in the scene. If you had a skeleton set up with feet controls you could add attributes which would control the pointing of the toes and the bending of the knees. When you start animating, you can use your designated control objects for all the keyframing.

How to add custom attributes

The first method for adding custom attributes is through the user interface. You can choose to add an attribute from either the main **Modify** menu or through the **Attributes** menu in the Attribute Editor.

1 **Add a new attribute to a primitive sphere**

- Create a primitive sphere.

- Select **Modify** → **Add Attribute...** or, in the Attribute Editor, select **Attributes** → **Add Attributes...**

  The **Add Attribute** window comes up, where you can define the new attribute.

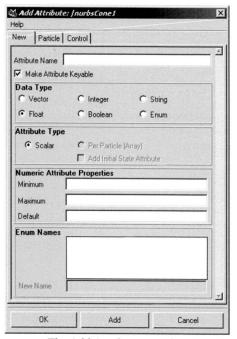

The Add Attributes window

2 Define the attribute

- Click the **New** tab and type in a name for the new attribute.

- If you want the attribute to show up in the Channel Box, it must be keyable.

   Make Attribute Keyable checked **On**.

   (**Data type** and **Attribute Type** will be discussed later.)

- Leave the **Min/Max/Default** fields blank.

   These fields let you set values for the initial value of the attribute and the minimum, maximum values that can be entered. If nothing is entered the default value is 0 and there is no minimum or maximum.

- Click **OK** to add the attribute and close the window.

   If you needed to add more attributes then you would click **Add**. The **Add** button adds the attribute and clears the fields so another attribute can be added.

Using MEL to add attributes

The second method for adding attributes is using the `addAttr` MEL command. The command becomes even more useful when several attributes need to be added to an object.

Common addAttr flags
-dv -defaultValue
-n -name
-ln -longName
-sn -shortName
-max -maxValue
-min -minValue
-k -keyable

Syntax

```
addAttr [flags] object
```

Tip: There are two flags for naming the attribute: `-shortName` and `-longName`. At least one of them must be used with the `addAttr` command.

Example

```
addAttr -longName "goForward" -shortName "gfwd";
```

This command creates an attribute on the active object with a long name of *goForward* and a short name of *gfwd*.

Note: This attribute will NOT be displayed in the Channel Box since we did not specify that it was a keyable attribute. The default value of the `-keyable` flag when it is not specified is OFF.

Example: Creating a lighting control node

To explore adding attributes, you will now open an existing scene and create a control node to control the lighting in a scene.

1 Open an existing scene file

- Open the file *02.AddAttrLights.ma*.
- Open the Outliner or the Hypergraph, and look at the scene contents.

2 Create a locator node

- Select **Create → Locator**.

   This locator is going to be used for setting up some attributes which will control the intensity of the lighting in the scene. You could use any other object to have your controls on, but a locator is just easier to select and will not render.

- Rename *locator1* to *lightControl*.
- Move *lightControl* above the scene geometry.

Tip: Use **Window** → **General Editors** → **Channel Control** window to move the transform attributes out of the keyable list and into the non-keyable list. This way the only attributes you will see are the light controls.

---

3 Add attributes to the null node

- Select the *lightControl* node.

- Enter the following commands:

```
addAttr -keyable true -shortName "fr" -longName
    "frontInt";

addAttr -keyable true -shortName "hb" -longName
    "highBackInt";

addAttr -keyable true -shortName "lb" -longName
    "lowBackInt";

addAttr -keyable false -shortName "ext" -longName
    "extra";
```

Boolean values

Value meaning TRUE: on, yes, true, 1 and any non-0 number.

Value meaning FALSE: off, no, false, 0

Tip: You can speed up your workflow by typing one line and then copy/paste the new line and make minor changes.

You now have a control object and the attributes for controlling the light intensities. You now need to make the control attributes actually control something in the scene. Right now they're not *connected* and don't control anything yet. You will be connecting them to the attributes they are meant to control in step 6.

4 Modifying an attribute with `setattr`

Notice the `extra` attribute does not show up in the Channel Box since its keyable flag was false. The `setAttr` command can be executed to modify an existing attribute. We will make the *extra* attribute keyable, so it shows up in the Channel Box.

- Enter the following commands:

```
setAttr -keyable true lightControl.extra;
```

The `-keyable` flag is for changing the keyable state of the attribute. Once it is keyable, then it will appear in the Channel Box.

5 Use MEL to delete attributes

If some attributes were added and they were no longer needed or were named incorrectly, they can be deleted using the `deleteAttr` command.

- Enter the following command:

```
deleteAttr -attribute "extra" lightControl;
```

This command removes the attribute.

6 Connect the new attributes to the intensity of the scene's lights

- Execute the following commands:

```
connectAttr lightControl.frontInt
    frontLightShape.intensity;

connectAttr lightControl.highBackInt
    highBackShape.intensity;

connectAttr lightControl.lowBackInt
    lowBackShape.intensity;
```

You have now connected the control attributes to their corresponding attributes in the scene.

This example shows how you can create an object, add attributes, and connect them to control other objects. This creates a faster workflow since one object controls multiple objects.

USING THE ADDED ATTRIBUTES

You can adjust the control object attributes with the Attribute Editor. The Attribute Editor displays the added attributes in the **Extra Attributes** section. Each attribute has its own text box for entering a value. If you would have specified a minimum and a maximum value with `addAttr`, sliders would have been created automatically beside the text field.

Using added attributes in the Attribute Editor

You will now open the Attribute Editor for the selected object, in this case, the *lightControl* object. Then you'll set values for the newly added attributes in the Attribute Editor.

1 View the attributes added to the control object

- Select the *lightControl* object.
- Select **Window** → **Attribute Editor**.
- Click on **Extra Attributes** to display the Extra Attributes section.

2 Edit the new attribute values

- Over the Maya workspace, press the **7** key to turn on hardware lighting and shading if it is not already enabled.
- Change the values of the *lightControl*'s lighting attributes to adjust the lighting levels.

Additional commands related to nodes and attributes

Up to this point you have seen some of the most commonly used commands related to attributes in Maya. Next, you will explore three commands that provide you with information about how specific nodes and attributes are related. You will continue to use the *addAttr.lights.ma* file to see some example usage of the following commands:

listRelatives: Used to obtain and traverse hierarchical information

listConnections: Displays attribute connection info for specified objects

ls: Provide a listing of information about the scene or a specific object

listRelatives

The **Scene Hierarchy** mode of the **Hypergraph** displays a graphical view of hierarchical (parent/child) relationships between objects in the scene. The *listRelatives* MEL command lets you tap into this information from the command line or a script.

- Type the following in the Script Editor:

```
select "topWin";
```

- Open **Window → Hypergraph** and press **f** hotkey to frame the selected object. You'll see parent child relationship of this particular object.
- Enter the following command in the Script Editor and view the printed results.

```
listRelatives -children "topWin";
```

- Execute the following to see a complete listing of other *listRelatives* flags.

```
help listRelatives;
```

listConnections

The **Dependency Graph** mode of the **Hypergraph** displays a graphical depiction of the attribute connections between nodes in the scene. The *listConnections* command is used to access this same information using MEL.

- Type the following:

```
select "hullShade";
```

- In the Hypergraph select **Graph → Input and Output Connections.**

- Move your mouse pointer over the arrow connections between the different nodes to display which attributes are connected.

- Enter the following command in the Script Editor and view the printed results:

```
listConnections -connections on "hullShade";
```

- View and experiment with the other flags available with *listConnections* to see the different results they produce (type *help listConnections* for a listing).

ls

It is very common that you will want to get a list of only certain elements in the scene so you can perform some operation to them. The *ls* command provides this powerful filtering functionality.

- Type the following:

```
ls -showType "frontLightShape";
```

- The result printed is the name of the object you specified followed by the *type* that Maya associates with that object. In this case it is telling you *frontLightShape* is a directional light.

- Type the following:

```
ls -type "directionalLight";
```

- The above prints out a list of all three directional lights in the scene. This functionality becomes very powerful once combined with variables and looping structures which will be discussed in detail later in this book.

- View and experiment with the other flags available with the *ls* command. Keep in mind that not all objects in Maya have a distinct type associated with them. If such a thing happens to you, *untyped* will be returned.

Exercises

To test what you have learned so far, complete the following exercises:

1 Using `listattr, getattr, setattr, aliasattr, listrelatives, listconnections, ls`

- Open the file *02.Train.ma*.

- Determine the train's current position and orientation.

- Change the position and orientation so that the train can move on the track.

- Make an alias called *forward* to control the train's movement on the track.

- Make any attributes that are not needed non-keyable so they are not displayed in the channel box.

- Print a listing of all *phongE* shaders in the scene, then select them using MEL commands.

- Save your work.

2 Make a thermometer

- Open the file *02.Thermometer.ma*.

  The scene consists of two curves (*bottomCurve* and *topCurve*) that are lofted together (*mercury*). Moving the *topCurve* will change the height of the *mercury*. There is a shader called *temperature* applied to the *mercury*.

- Use the appropriate MEL commands to make the color of the mercury change from black to red as the height of the mercury rises.

- Make the control as obvious as possible. Depending on the graphics card in your computer, you may have to render a frame in order to see the results.

- Save your work.

Tip: The multiply/divide utility node can be used to change the range that the temperature works over.

---

3 Using `connectattr` and `disconnectattr`

- Open the file from exercise 1, *02.Train.ma*.

- Connect the rotation of the front wheel to the three rear wheels on each side so that only one wheel needs to be animated.

- Save your work.

4 Modify a control box

- Open the file *02.TrainControl.ma*.

- Delete or disable the display of any irrelevant attributes in the Channel Box.

- Add attributes to the *ControlBox* node to control the rotation of the levers.

Key objectives covered

You now have an understanding of how attributes work and how they are affected by various MEL commands. Since attributes are so important to Maya's dependency graph, you will be working with them a great deal.

The following key concepts were covered in this chapter:

- Viewing attributes using the Channel Box and the Attribute Editor.

- MEL commands that allow you to work with attributes:

```
listAttr

getAttr

setAttr

aliasAttr
```

- How to connect attributes using the Connection Editor.

- MEL commands for connecting and disconnecting attributes:

```
connectAttr

disconnectAttr
```

- Adding attributes with the Attribute Editor.

- MEL commands for adding and deleting attributes:

```
addAttr

deleteAttr
```

- MEL commands for traversing nodes and listing information:

```
listConnections
listRelatives
ls
```

3 Commands and Syntax

In the previous lessons you were using simple MEL commands in the Script Editor. To further understand MEL commands, the command structure will be explored. It is important to lay down a few ground rules for entering MEL commands to make it easier to read and edit your scripts at a later time.

In this lesson you will look at:

- The general structure of a MEL command.

- How to Create, Edit, and Query using the MEL commands.

- Some initial syntax rules to help you as you start writing scripts.

CHAPTER 3

MEL COMMAND STRUCTURE

Most of the MEL commands in Maya have the same general structure:

```
command -flags "name";
```

The first word is the actual command you want to execute. The second word with a dash in front of it represents the flags for that command. A command flag allows you to explicitly define how the command will be executed by specifying argument(s). The last word, *"name"*, represents the internal name that Maya will hold for the results of that command or the name of the object the command is executed on. Not all MEL commands have *name* of *flag* in their structure, for example:

```
sphere;
```

When the above command is executed, Maya reads the line until it hits a semi-colon. The semi-colon signifies the end of the command.

```
sphere -pivot 8 4 7;
```

The first word "sphere" tells Maya to execute the sphere command. The next word "-pivot" is a valid flag for the sphere command telling Maya that we want to specify where the pivot point for the new sphere will be located. It is then followed by the arguments of that flag, in this case, the pivot's xyz.

When the following window command is executed Maya will create a window with a title of *First Window*. "myWin" is the name that Maya will use to keep track of this window. You could run the window command without the word myWin on the end. If you did this then Maya would give the window its own internal name.

```
window -title "First Window" myWin;
```

Create, Edit, and Query using the MEL commands

Commands in Maya have three different modes of execution. There is *Create*, *Edit*, and *Query*. Each command is different in Maya and not all of them are able to work in each of the three modes. If you look in the on-line documentation you will see that some of the commands have some combination of *C*, *E*, or *Q*. These letters are associated with the flags for the command.

If you look at the loft command in Create mode, it creates a nurbs surface between two or more curves.

```
loft curve1 curve2;
// Result: loftedSurface1 loft1 //
```

Note: Commands by default are in Create mode. They don't need any special flags. To put a command in edit or query mode the -edit and -query flags are used.

If you were unsure of what degree the surface was, you could use the loft command and put it in query mode.

```
loft -query -degree loft1;
```

When the above command is executed, Maya reads the first word `loft` and then the flag `-query` which tells Maya to put the loft command in query mode. When a command is in query mode the next flag encountered will be queried. In this case it is `-degree`. The last word in the command is the name of the object to be queried.

```
// Result: 3 //
```

You now know that the surface is degree 3.

If you wanted to change the surface degree you could put the command in edit mode.

```
loft -edit -degree 1 loft1;
// Result: Values edited. //
```

This command will edit the `loft1` surface and change the surface degree to 1. Again, notice the structure. The first word is the command `loft` and the first flag is `-edit` which puts the command in edit mode. The next flag is what will be edited on the surface followed by its new value. The last word is the name of the surface to perform the edit upon.

Note: In most cases, if the object is selected you don't need to include the object name in the command e.g. `loft -edit -degree 1` will change the surface degree of the active loft surface.

MEL SYNTAX

You also need to be aware of some simple syntax rules. When you start writing multiple MEL commands it can be difficult to read if things aren't formatted properly. It can also be difficult for others to read your scripts and for you to go back and edit your own if the formatting is poor.

Semicolons

All MEL commands end with a semicolon. This is a very common error. If you have executed several lines of MEL and ran into an error, check to make sure that each MEL command has a semicolon.

Flag Names

Avoid using the short form for command flags. If someone else will be working on your script they will have to spend time looking up the flags to see their meaning. Take the time to include the full name of the flag the first time around.

The flags below are difficult to understand:

```
select -adn;

revolve -ulp curve1;
```

The long forms have more meaning:

```
select -allDependencyNodes;

revolve -useLocalPivot curve1;
```

White Space

Use lots of white space to break up commands, flags, and programming structures. White space includes spaces, tab characters, and blank lines. White space has no effect on the execution of a script but it can greatly improve the readability.

```
curve -p 0 0 0 -p 2 1 0 -p -2 2 0 -p 0 3 0;rename
"loftCurve";for($x=0;$x<6;$x++){duplicate;move -r $x 1
2;}select -all;loft;for($x=0;$x<12;$x++)
{duplicate;rotate -r 0 30 0;}
```

The above script has no regard for white space and makes it extremely difficult to read. If you add some white space and some line breaks, you will be able to understand it better.

```
curve -p 0 0 0 -p 2 1 0 -p -2 2 0 -p 0 3 0;

rename "loftCurve";

for ($x = 0; $x < 6; $x++)
{
    duplicate;
    move -r $x 1 2;
}
select -all;
```

```
loft;
for ($x = 0; $x < 12; $x++)
{
   duplicate;
   rotate -r 0 30 0;
}
```

Comments

Add comments to your MEL commands for explaining what is happening. This is invaluable for yourself and others. When you will go back to a script tomorrow, in a week, or in a year, you want to be able to remember what you were doing at the time. The same thing applies if you pass your scripts on to others; they will also be able to understand it.

There are two ways to add comments. For a single line comment, use two forward slashes (//). For a comment that will be more than a single line, use a forward slash, asterisk combination (/* comments in here */). These methods can also be used to comment out certain lines if you don't want them to be executed.

```
//Create a curve with four control vertices
curve -p 0 0 0 -p 2 1 0 -p -2 2 0 -p 0 3 0;
rename "loftCurve"; //new name for the curve


//Use a for loop to create several curves
for ($x = 0; $x < 6; $x++)
{
   duplicate;
   move -r $x 1 2;
}

/*
Once the curves are created select them all and loft
them to form a surface
*/
select -all;
loft;
```

```
/*Use another for loop to create several surfaces and
rotate them about their pivot point*/
for ($x = 0; $x < 12; $x++)
{
   duplicate;
   rotate -r 0 30 0;
}
//print "This command is commented.";
```

Multiple Line Commands

When Maya is reading a MEL command, it determines the end of the command by a semicolon regardless of how many lines are used. Some MEL commands have so many flags that a single command will be wider than your Script Editor. This makes it very difficult to read. If you move the flags to different lines then you improve the readability. In the following MEL commands, notice the scrollLayout command covers several lines:

```
window -widthHeight 350 150;
   scrollLayout
         -width 200
         -height 250
         -horizontalScrollBarThickness 16
         -verticalScrollBarThickness    16
         -childResizable true;
      rowColumnLayout
            -numberOfColumns 3;
      int $index;
      for ($index = 0; $index < 10; $index++)
      {
         text;
         intField;
         intSlider;
      }
showWindow;
```

Key objectives covered

In order to have a better understanding of MEL commands, we have looked at a few important concepts. This helps lay the groundwork for better MEL usage and script writing as we learn more. The following key concepts were covered in this chapter:

- MEL command structure
- *Create, Edit,* and *Query* command modes
- MEL syntax

Creating Custom UI

One of the most powerful ways MEL can streamline your workflow is by creating a custom user interface (UI) designed specifically for your needs.

Examples of situations that you might want to create a custom UI for are limitless. You can have windows, scroll lists, radio buttons, sliders, list boxes, buttons, check boxes, etc. For example, you could have a button that will put a dragon's face in a certain pose, have a checkbox that will skin a skeleton, create a slider that moves an object along a path, or another control for anything else that you can dream up.

You will see how easily custom UI can be created by building some custom controls. First, you will look at a recipe formula for creating custom UI. With this recipe, you can cut and paste to create custom UI. You will then look at how to manage the windows you create and how to query and edit windows to find out if they exist or change their appearance. You will also look at a window example with multiple layouts to help you understand a more complex window setup.

The topics covered in this section are:

- Creating a simple window and adding UI elements

- Window management commands

- Querying or Editing UI elements

- Multiple layouts and the `setParent` command

CREATING SIMPLE UI CONTROLS

The first step to creating a simple UI of your own is to create a window for it to appear in. Using MEL is like *telling* Maya what you want it to do.

Create a window using MEL

- Execute the following in the Script Editor:

```
window;

showWindow;
```

The first line creates a generic window object. The second line displays the last window created.

Generic window object

- Grab a corner of the window and resize it.

  You'll see that you've just created an empty window. This window comes with the standard motif features such as the ability to resize, minimize, and expand it. You also get the motif window menu for performing several window actions.

Create a window using the title flag

Now you will name the window, *myWindow*. To do this, you will modify the way you use the `window` command by using one of its many flags.

- Execute the following in the Script Editor:

```
window -title "My Window";
showWindow;
```

This time, when the window appears, it is named *My Window*. Every command in Maya has many flags which you can use to modify the way the command is executed. The flag `-title` lets you name the window.

The help command

In addition to the on-line documentation, you can also get help from Maya directly using the `help` command.

- Type the following to get help on the `window` command.

Common window flags

-e -edit

-q -query

-w -width

-h -height

-wh -widthHeight

-s -sizeable

-t -title

Help command

`help commandName;` gives you a short description of the commandName.

`help -doc "command";` opens up a web browser with the command information.

`help -list "*text";` searches for a pattern "text" represents the letters that will be used in the search. * is a wildcard.

```
help window;
```

Maya returns a list of all the flags for that command. This is a great way to find out how to use a command without having to remember what every command does.

Tip: You can access the on-line docs for a command with `help -doc "window";`.

A window with a title and an internal name

When a window is created with the `-title` flag, the title is present in the title bar of the window. This title is purely for visual purposes. Maya doesn't refer to the window using that title. Maya will automatically create a name that it will use internally to refer to this window. To help keep track of the windows you are creating, it is a good idea to specify a name for Maya to use internally for future reference. After creating the window you may need to delete the window or check for it's existence and this is possible only if you know what the window is called.

- Execute the following in the Script Editor:

```
window -title "My Window" myWin;

showWindow;
```

You'll notice that the window command reflects the MEL command structure of `command -flags name`. The last word in the command, `myWin`, has given the window an internal name. You will now be able to access this window using that name. If you don't include the `-title` flag or a name for the window, Maya will create a default name that will show up in the window title bar.

Adding a layout and a button

Now that you have learned how to create a window, it's time to put something in it. The things you put in windows are known as UI elements. You will begin by adding a button.

Before you start adding things into the window, it may be helpful to think of the `window` and `showWindow` commands as bookends. Everything you put between these two commands will appear in the window.

To create a button, you will use the `button` command. Before you use this command, you will also require the `columnLayout` command. Whenever you want to add things to a window, you need to tell the window how to organize the items. This is referred to as the layout of the window.

Window layouts

A window must have at least one layout in order to add other UI elements like buttons and sliders. If one isn't present when you attempt to add a UI element, you will get an error similar to this:

```
// Error: line 2:
Controls must have a
layout.
```

```
No layout found in
window: window1 //
```

If this happens, execute the `showWindow` command to make the window visible and then close the window. Always make sure to add a layout following the window command.

- Enter the following into the Script Editor:

```
window -title "My Window";
columnLayout;
button;
showWindow;
```

Now you have a window with a button in it.

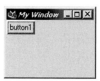

A window with a button

Some columnLayout flags

-adj	adjustableColumn
-h	height
-w	width
-cw	columnWidth
-rs	rowSpacing

In MEL, there are several different types of layouts which you can use for a window. Each type gives you different sorts of control for organizing the items in your window. The easiest of these to use is the `columnLayout`. This command simply puts everything in a column from the top of your window to the bottom and stacks them on top of one another. It's a great organizing command for beginning MEL scripting because it doesn't require any additional setup.

Other common types of layouts are `formLayout`, `scrollLayout`, `frameLayout` and `rowLayout`. `FormLayout` gives you the most control but it is also more difficult to use.

Tip: A window can have one or more different layouts which are needed to add controls or UI elements. You might use several different layouts to further customize the look of your window. One layout alone can be very restricting for positioning window controls or UI elements.

A window which contains four buttons

- Enter the following into the Script Editor:

```
window -title "My Window";
columnLayout;
    button;
    button;
    button;
    button -label "Test";
showWindow;
```

Some button flags

-l	label
-h	height
-w	width
-c	command

The `columnLayout` command is able to organize the buttons in the window.

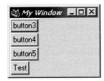

A window with four buttons

Using the `columnLayout` tells Maya to place all the UI elements (in this case, buttons) in a column. Without a layout command, you will get an error saying:

```
// Error: line 2: Controls must have a layout. No
layout found in window
```

Now that you have successfully added buttons to the window, you can make them do something. You will use the `-command` flag to attach a command to the button. Any MEL command or script can be referenced here. Here's a simple example:

A window with a button that creates a sphere

- Enter the following into the Script Editor:

```
window -title "My Window";

columnLayout;

    button -label "Make a Sphere" -command "sphere";

showWindow;
```

Now, everytime you push the button, the `sphere` command is executed. Try some more buttons with other commands.

WINDOW MANAGEMENT

Once you start creating numerous UI elements, you will need to be aware of some commands for helping you to manage those elements.

Listing UI elements

A problem that everyone encounters when creating UI is creating too many windows and getting errors saying that the name you are trying to create is not unique. The solution to the problem is to list all the existing windows with the following command:

```
lsUI -windows
```

Some of the other flags for this command are as follows:

`-panels`	List all currently existing panels
`-editors`	List all currently existing editors
`-controls`	List controls created using ELF UI commands (e.g. buttons, checkBoxes, etc.)
`-menus`	List menus created using ELF UI commands
`-menuItems`	List menu items created using ELF UI commands

1 Create several windows

- Enter the following into the Script Editor:

```
window -title "My Window";
   columnLayout;
   button;
window -title "Another Window";
   columnLayout;
   button;
window -title "Last Window";
   columnLayout;
   button;
showWindow;
```

When this is executed, you will notice that the only window that shows up is the last window created since you have only one `showWindow` call. How do you get the other windows to show up? Since you don't know the names of the windows created, you can use the `lsUI -windows` command.

- Enter the following into the Script Editor:

```
lsUI -windows;
```

Once this has been executed, you will be able to see the names of all the windows in your scene (listed alphabetically). The default name the window command gives a window is "window1", "window2", "window3", etc. The windows you just created should be the last few names on the list.

- Enter the following into the Script Editor (substitute the proper window names from the `lsUI` command):

```
showWindow "window1";
showWindow "window2";
```

Note: If you have named your windows properly, then it is easy to make them visible with the `showWindow` command. You won't need to go through the extra step of listing the existing windows.

Naming UI elements

As mentioned above, naming UI elements can make things easier. With any UI element, the name can be specified at the end of the command.

```
command -flags name;
```

Remember the window that was created above had a button to make a sphere. It can be rewritten as follows so that all the UI elements are named:

```
window -title "My Window" sphereWindow;
    columnLayout firstLayout;
        button -label "Make a Sphere"
                -command "sphere"
                sphereButton;
showWindow sphereWindow;
```

Naming UI elements will be very important as you write more complex scripts. With the elements named, you can query and edit them to make your scripts more robust.

Deleting UI elements

UI Elements are deleted using the `deleteUI` command.

For example, executing the command after running the simple window below, will delete the button:

```
window winName;
columnLayout;
button -label "Button Label" buttonName;
showWindow;
```

Now use the following to remove the button:

```
deleteUI buttonName;
```

Executing the following command will delete the window and its content:

```
deleteUI winName;
```

Note:	Closing a window deletes the window and any UI elements that were in it, unless you use the `window -retain` command. Using this flag will cause Maya to retain the window in memory. The only way to delete the window is with the `deleteUI` command.

Querying or Editing UI elements

Existing UI elements can also be queried and edited, without rebuilding the entire UI. As long as you name the elements in a UI, they can be queried or edited.

1 Create a simple window with a button

- Enter the following in the Script Editor:

```
window -title "Test Window" winName;

columnLayout;

button -label "Button Test" -w 50 buttonName;

showWindow;
```

- Use the following to change the button:

```
button -edit -w 200 buttonName;
```

When editing a control or a window you must always include the `-edit` flag and the name of the element.

2 Query a window to see if it exists

- Enter the following in the Script Editor:

```
window -title "Test Window" winName;
columnLayout;
button -label "Button Test" -w 50 buttonName;
showWindow;
```

- Use the window command in query mode to see if the window exists:

```
window -query -exists winName;
```

This will return 1 or 0 for true or false. This illustrates two things. The first is why it is important to name UI elements. If you don't know the name of the object you can't query or edit it. The second is determining if a UI has been created. This becomes more important later when you are creating custom UI with scripts. You want to be able to verify the existence of a UI element so you can either query or edit it.

3 Create a window and query its position

If you want to be able to create a window and position it at a specific position, you need to know the coordinates of this position. In order to find this out, create a window and move it to the position you want. Then query the window and ask where it is located. One flag you can use is -topLeftCorner.

- Enter the following in the Script Editor:

```
window -title "Position Me" winCoordinates;
showWindow
```

- Position the window where you want it to show up and enter the following in the Script Editor:

```
window -query -topLeftCorner winCoordinates;
```

This command will return the coordinates of the top left corner. You can then use these coordinates in conjunction with the window -edit flag to place the window in the same position whenever it is created.

- Create a window with some UI elements and use the coordinates from the previous example for positioning:

```
window myWin;
columnLayout;
button;
window -edit -topLeftCorner 300 420 myWin;
showWindow myWin;
```

When you want to place a window in a specific position you need to write the MEL commands in a specific order. The first command will be the window command with a proper name. The next commands are any layouts, buttons, controls etc. The last thing you do is add a window -edit command before the showWindow command. This ensures that the window will be in the correct position, or the correct size before display, eliminating flickers.

OTHER UI ELEMENTS

You have now explored how to create a window with the simplest of UI elements. To expand what you can do with the custom user interface, we will add some slider bars to control the levers in the *TrainControl* file.

For this example, you will use a command called `attrFieldSliderGroup`. This command creates a complete slider and text field and connects it to an object in your scene. This is another example where MEL simplifies your scripting by requiring only one command to create a sophisticated UI element. You will recreate the previous button script with the `attrFieldSliderGrp` command.

How to create a slider

1 Open the file

- Open the file *04.TrainControl.ma*.

  You'll be using this example scene to create your own custom UI with sliders, checkboxes, buttons, and other UI elements.

2 Create a window with slider and a value field

- Enter the following into the Script Editor:

```
window -title "My Window";
columnLayout;
    attrFieldSliderGrp -min 0 -max 85
        -attribute LeftLever.rotateX;
showWindow;
```

New window with slider

When the window appears, you'll be able to control the first lever with the slider. Take a look at the command you used. Instead of `button` you used `attrFieldSliderGrp`. You also added in two flags for the `min` and `max` values for the slider. The most important part of the command is the `-attribute` flag. This tells the slider which object and attribute it is connected to.

3 Create a window with 3 attribute sliders

You will now redo the script to make 3 sliders. You can just copy and paste what you've already done and change the names to work properly.

- Enter the following into the Script Editor:

```
window -title "My Window";

columnLayout;

    attrFieldSliderGrp -label "Lever 1" -min 0 -max 85
        -at LeftLever.rx;

    attrFieldSliderGrp -label "Lever 2" -min 0 -max 85
        -at MiddleLever.rx;

    attrFieldSliderGrp -label "Lever 3" -min 0 -max 85
        -at RightLever.rx;

showWindow;
```

Some common attrFieldSliderGrp flags	
-e	edit
-q	query
-l	label
-h	height
-w	width
-at	attribute
-min	minValue
-max	maxValue
-s	step
-fmn	fieldMinValue
-fmx	fieldMaxValue
-fs	fieldStep
-smn	sliderMinValue
-smx	sliderMaxValue
-ss	sliderStep

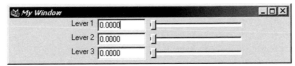

New window with 3 attribute sliders

Now you have a window with controls for positioning the levers. Notice how you've added a label flag to each slider and used the short version of the attribute flag (-at). Most flags have an abbreviated form so that you don't have to write them out every time.

Another useful feature of the attrFieldSliderGrp is the **RMB** menu. Simply hold down the **RMB** over the field next to the slider and you will get a menu which will allow you to set a keyframe, write an expression, or map a texture to the given attribute. Again, MEL has let you use a simple command to get a lot of user interface control.

4 Create a window with a checkbox and 3 sliders

Next, you will add a checkbox. The checkbox is a great UI element to learn how to use because it demonstrates how you can have a different command happen whenever you turn something on or off. The command for checkbox is checkBox. You will add a checkbox to control the incandescence of one of the little lights.

- Enter the following into the Script Editor:

```
window -title "My Window";

columnLayout;

    attrFieldSliderGrp -label "Lever 1"
                        -min 0 -max 85
                        -attribute LeftLever.rx;
```

```
attrFieldSliderGrp -label "Lever 2"
                        -min 0 -max 85
                        -attribute MiddleLever.rx;
attrFieldSliderGrp -label "Lever 3"
                        -min 0 -max 85
                        -attribute RightLever.rx;
checkBox -l "Red Light"
    -onCommand "setAttr blinn1.incandescence 1 0 0;"
    -offCommand "setAttr blinn1.incandescence 0 0 0;";

showWindow;
```

Some checkBox flags

-l label

-h height

-w width

-cc changeCommand

-ofc offCommand

-onc onCommand

-v value

New window with checkbox

Tip: Don't forget to resize the window to see the checkbox.

Try the checkbox. As you click it on and off, the red light should turn on and off on the Train Controls. You used two flags to accomplish this; the -onCommand and the -offCommand. The onCommand is executed when the checkbox is turned on while the offCommand is executed when the checkbox is turned off.

By going to the Hypershade and changing the values for each shader's incandescence, you are able to find out exactly what the right command is to change the color of the shader. The 3 numbers after the attributes represent Red, Green, and Blue values. Try adding more checkboxes for the other two lightBulbs.

Tip: Check out the checkBoxGrp command in the on-line docs. It gives you even more control for placing checkboxes but requires a little more setup.

Adding text and separators

As you continue constructing a custom UI, you will often find it necessary to label and organize your button, sliders, etc. In addition to the -label or -

`title` flags which many UI elements have, you can also use a text UI element. It is very easy to use. You simply type:

```
text -label "Your text here";
```

Another trick is to use an empty text UI element to just add a space between UI elements in your layout.

```
text -l "";
```

1 Add labels to your window

Using the text UI element, add some labels to the different parts of your UI.

- Enter the following into the Script Editor:

```
window -title "My Window";
columnLayout;


    text -label "Lever Controls";
    attrFieldSliderGrp -l "Lever 1"
                        -min 0 -max 85
                        -at LeftLever.rx;
    attrFieldSliderGrp -l "Lever 2"
                        -min 0 -max 85
                        -at MiddleLever.rx;
    attrFieldSliderGrp -l "Lever 3"
                        -min 0 -max 85
                        -at RightLever.rx;
    text -label "";
    text -label "";
    text -label "Light Controls";


    checkBox -l "Red Light"
        -onCommand "setAttr blinn1.ic 1 0 0;"
        -offCommand "setAttr blinn1.ic 0 0 0;";
showWindow;
```

Some text flags

-l label

-al align

-h height

-w width

Align is the alignment of the text. Align can be "left", "right", or "center".

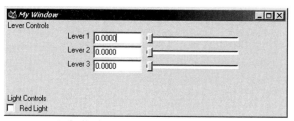

Labelled windows and UI elements

Some separator flags

-l label

-st style

-h height

-w width

Style is the look of the separator. Style can be: "none","single", "double","singleDash", "doubleDash","in" or "out".

2 Add a separator between parts of your window

In addition to text, you can also add separators to your UI. Separators are lines which divide up the space in a window. For this window, you will add a separator right before the light controls.

- Enter the following into the Script Editor:

```
window -title "My Window";
  columnLayout;
    text -label "Lever Controls";
      attrFieldSliderGrp -l "Lever 1"
                    -min 0 -max 85
                    -at LeftLever.rx;
      attrFieldSliderGrp -l "Lever 2"
                    -min 0 -max 85
                    -at MiddleLever.rx;
      attrFieldSliderGrp -l "Lever 3"
                    -min 0 -max 85
                    -at RightLever.rx;
    text -label "";
    separator -width 400;
    text -label "";

    text -label "Light Controls";
    checkBox -l "Red Light"
      -onCommand "setAttr blinn1.ic 1 0 0;"
      -offCommand "setAttr blinn1.ic 0 0 0;";
  showWindow;
```

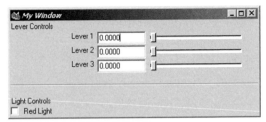

Window with a separator

There are several different styles of separators including dotted lines and double lines. Check out the on-line docs for examples with these different styles.

Multiple layouts and the setParent command

Every window needs a layout and if you want to have effectively designed customized windows you need to understand how to use more than one layout at a time. When you start dealing with multiple layouts, you also need to understand the parent child relationship that is created and how to navigate around it.

To navigate from one UI element to another you can use the `setParent` command. This command allows you to change from one parent to another by specifying the name of the parent. Once you have used the `setParent` command, you are able to add new UI elements to the specified parent.

1 Create 3 windows

In this example, you will create several empty windows and make them visible. After they are visible you will start adding some controls.

- Enter the following in the Script Editor:

```
window first;
showWindow;
window second;
showWindow;
window third;
showWindow
```

You may need to move the windows around since they might be created on top of each other.

Layout examples

The on-line documentation has numerous layout examples. Press **F1** to bring up the help web browser. Go to the *MEL User Guide* and choose *Creating Interfaces*. These examples will provide you with a starting point for understanding the different layout types.

You can also go in the *MEL Command Reference* and select `frameLayout` for example. Scroll to the bottom of the page, you will find some examples for that command.

To see a list of all the available Layouts: `help -list "*Layout";`

2 Add a layout and a button to each window

Now that you have created the windows use the `setParent` command to go to a specific window and then add a layout and a button.

- Execute the following lines one at a time:

```
setParent first;
columnLayout;
   button;
setParent third;
columnLayout;
   button;
setParent second;
   button;
```

The last line should result in an error. You need to add a layout before you can add other UI elements.

When you create a window, Maya by default makes that window the parent of any controls (buttons, layouts) that are added until another new window is created. At the same time, when you have created a window and then a layout (e.g. `columnLayout`), the layout is a child of the window and a parent of any new controls that are added. If you add another layout, this new layout will be a child of the first layout and so on. If you wanted it to be a child of the window you would have to tell Maya who the parent is.

3 Create a window with multiple layouts

- Enter the following MEL commands in the Script Editor. Highlight and execute the commands one at a time and watch the history field of the Script Editor for the result of each command after execution.

Note: The script for this example exists in the on-line documentation for the layout command: `frameLayout`

```
window;
```

Highlight window in the Script Editor and execute it. In the history field of the Script Editor you will see the following result:

```
// Result: window1 //
```

- Continue working through these MEL commands one at a time:

```
scrollLayout scrollLayout;
```

```
columnLayout -adjustableColumn true;
    frameLayout -label "Buttons"
        -labelAlign "top"
        -borderStyle "in";
/* Remember that a command can span more than one
line. Look for the semicolon for the end of a
command. */
            columnLayout;
                button;
                button;
                button;
                setParent ..;
            setParent ..;
        frameLayout -label "Scroll Bars"
            -labelAlign "center"
            -borderStyle "out";
            columnLayout;
                intSlider;
                intSlider;
                intSlider;
                setParent ..;
            setParent ..;
        frameLayout -label "Fields"
            -labelAlign "center"
            -borderStyle "etchedIn";
            columnLayout;
                intField;
                intField;
                intField;
                setParent ..;
            setParent ..;
        frameLayout -label "Check Boxes"
            -labelAlign "bottom"
            -borderStyle "etchedOut";
            columnLayout;
```

```
                        checkBox;

                        checkBox;

                        checkBox;

                        setParent ..;

                setParent ..;

        showWindow;
```

What you will have noticed from watching the results of each of these UI commands is that you are creating a hierarchy of UI elements. As you execute them you are going deeper into the hierarchy. If you want to change to a different level, use the `setParent` command. After you added the 3 buttons, you needed to include the `setParent` command to move up two levels. The syntax for this command was "`setParent ..`" which tells Maya to move up one level in the UI hierarchy. That is why you needed the two `setParent` commands.

Tip: If you are naming your UI elements properly then instead of using `setParent ..` to navigate around you can specify the UI element by name. i.e. `setParent columnLayout1;`

A further illustration of the setParent command

- Using the script from the last example, add the collapsable flag on all the `frameLayout` commands.

```
        frameLayout -label "Buttons"

                -labelAlign "center"

                -collapsable true

                -borderStyle "in";
```

- Once you have added the collapsable flag to all the `frameLayout` commands, highlight and execute the script to create a window.

- Comment out all the `setParent` commands in the script by using the double forward slash.

```
        columnLayout;

                columnLayout;

                        button;

                        button;

                        button;

                        // setParent ..;
```

```
// setParent ..;
```

- Highlight and execute the script to create a second window.

  If you compare the windows side by side they look similar. If you start clicking on the collapse buttons starting from the bottom you will notice a difference. In the first window you will still see the labels for each `frameLayout`. In the second window the bottom layout is actually a child of the collapsable `frameLayout` above it. When you removed the `setParent` commands you removed the hierarchy effect and the layouts were added in a straight line.

Referencing the documentation

From the Help pull-down menu at the upper right side of the Maya interface, you can access the on-line documentation. Included in this documentation is an extensive section on UI commands, or ELF commands as they are referred to in the docs.

Each command or UI element has an example script at the end which you can just cut and paste directly into the Script Editor and execute to see an example of how it works.

This is probably the most interesting and interactive way to explore UI construction in MEL. It's also a great way to get pointed in the right direction when you're having trouble.

Continue working with the example scene and try using some of the UI elements and scene commands which haven't been talked about. If you get stuck, check out the example script in the documentation.

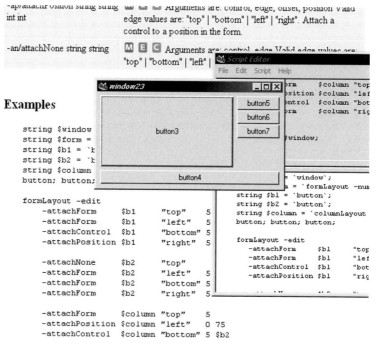

An example from the on-line documentation.

Exercises

1 Building UI

- Create a window that could be used to dial a telephone. Include all the numerical buttons, a field to show the number dialed, a volume control, and a button to show if the line is in use or not.

2 Create a control window for a person

- Open the file *04.Passenger.ma*.
- Create a window with controls to raise the person's arm and wave.
- Add controls for the direction he is looking in.

Summary

As you learn more about scripting and start writing some scripts of your own, you will know the importance of the UI command set. The ability to write custom UI will be of great benefit to you and make it easy to provide user interaction with your scripts.

This lesson will have provided you with the basics of understanding the UI command set as well as where to go for more UI information.

The topics covered in this section were:

- Creating a simple window and adding UI elements
- Window management commands
- Querying or Editing UI elements
- Multiple layouts and the `setParent` command

Additional information is available in the UI Appendix A of this manual.

5 Variables

Variables are an important aspect of working with MEL. They allow you to design more robust scripts that can work for multiple scenarios. If you created a script that takes the active object and duplicates it, without variables the name of the active object would have to be the same every time. In that case, a variable allows you to store the name of the active object and then work with that name to perform other commands. If the active object changes, the script will continue to work.

When you are scripting, it is always a good idea to establish the different variables that will play a role in your script. By starting with a variable, you can make sure that you are using descriptive names that make your script more readable.

Variables are also needed to hold values which are used repeatedly in a script or for values returned by a MEL command. If a value is used repeatedly in a script it can be assigned to a variable. This helps people understand where the number came from since they can read the variable name and if you later want to change the number then you only have to do it once at the beginning of the script.

In this lesson, you will learn the following;

- How to recognize different variable types
- How to declare a variable
- The naming convention
- How to assign a value to a variable
- The data-types conversion table
- The operator precedence
- How to capture the result of a command in a variable
- The `tokenize` command

VARIABLES

A variable is a storage place. You can think of it sort of like a drawer where you can keep numbers or letters or groups of both until you are ready to use them. Each drawer can only hold one type of object though. `Drawer1` could hold numbers while `Drawer2` might hold letters. When you create a variable, you must tell Maya what sort of things can be stored in it. There are several *types* of things you can store in a variable. They are called data types. The most common data types are *floats*, *integers*, *vectors*, and *strings*.

Floats and integers are very similar. They are both numbers. The only difference is that an integer must be a whole number or the negative opposites of whole numbers. That is, it cannot have a fraction or a decimal point. It's a number like 1, 10 or -50. A float can be any real number, whole or otherwise. An object's *translateX* would be expressed as a float since it could be any value like 1.32, -104.3 or 7.0.

Vectors are simply a collection of three numbers all in one. RGB values are expressed as vectors (<<Red, Green, Blue>>). For example, the color blue is expressed as <<0,0,1>>. Translation, rotation and scaling are vectors too. Vectors are always typed inside of double less-than and greater-than signs.

A string is a group of letters. It can be a letter, a word, or even a whole sentence. The names of objects are stored as strings. When you start making your own scripts, you'll use strings when you decide to name the objects your script is creating.

The following table shows four variable types:

Type	Meaning	Examples
int	integer (...-2, -1, 0, 1, 2...)	10, -5 or 0
float	fractional numbers	392.6, 7.0 or -2.667
vector	collection of 3 numbers (XYZ and RGB are example vectors)	<<1, 0, 1>> or <<-5.2, 2.45, -1.0>>
string	one or more characters	"What's up, chief?"

All variables in MEL begin with a dollar sign. Variable names cannot include spaces or special characters. You can use underscores and numbers as long as the variable name does not start with a number. Variable names are case sensitive. In other words, $temp is a different variable name than $Temp.

Declaring and assigning

Declaring a variable simply tells Maya that you have created a new drawer and defines what kind of data type it can hold. Assigning a variable means you've put something into that drawer. If you try to use a variable before it has been declared, you will get the following error:

```
// Error: Line 1.16: "$variable" is an undeclared
variable. //
```

Just remember that you can't use a drawer that you haven't created yet. Here's an example of how to declare several different types of variables.

Examples

```
int $Temp;
float $temp;
string $tEmp;
```

The examples below show how to assign values to the above declared variables. Use an equal sign to set the value for a variable. The variable to the left of the equal sign is assigned to the value to the right of the equal sign.

```
$Temp = 3;
$temp = 222.222;
$tEmp = "Heya kid.";
```

You can also declare and assign a variable in the same line.

Examples

```
string $howdy = "Howdy";

float $radius = 20.56;

int $hitch = 42;
```

In addition to declaring and assigning variables, you can perform different operations on them. You can add, subtract, or perform any other math function to modify or change their value. Try entering some of these examples into the Script Editor.

Examples

```
float $temp = 5.4;
$temp = $temp + 5; //(or $temp += 5;)
print $temp;
//Result: 10.4//
```

Variables

If a variable is declared with no assignment, all values are assigned 0, except for strings which are assigned empty quotation marks.

Example:

float $teMP;

Assigned 0;

string $TEMp;

Assigned "";

vector $TEmP;

Assigned <<0, 0, 0>>;

```
string $what = "Whale";
string $title = "Great" + " White " + $what;
print $title;
//Result: Great White Whale


string $name = "My Sphere";
float $radius = 5;
sphere -radius $radius -name $name;
// A sphere named "My Sphere" of radius 5 is created


string $what = "The beginning of ";
print ($what + "December\n");
//notice the print statement uses brackets, without
// them you would get an error.
```

Note:	The print command allows you to view the contents of a variable. The proper syntax is `print $variable`. The contents of the variable will be displayed in the history section of the Script Editor. To go to a new line in the history section of the Script Editor use the following syntax: `print "Hello\n";` In this case "\n" means new line. The back slash is an escape sequence. An escape sequence is a method to tell Maya that the character following it is special. **\n** creates a new line, **\t** creates tab, **** double slash tells the system that the second slash is to be treated like a normal character, **\"** tells the system that the quotation is to be treated like a normal character.

Naming convention

As you see in the above example, it can be hard to figure out the type of a variable only by its name. A naming convention is a way to name things in a script, such as variables, a specific way. For example, you may want all the variables to start with a company's initials, followed by an intuitive name. This way, it is easier to know if a variable comes from one of your scripts and what is its usage.

Next is a table specifying how we could name variables, depending on type.

Data types	Convention	Examples
int	i	$iTmp, $iNumber
float	f	$fTemp, $fSlider
vector	v	$vTest, $vTrans

Data types	Convention	Examples
string	none	$string, $text
global	g_	$g_iLoop, $g_fVal

Throughout this book, we will try to stick as much as possible to this naming convention.

Explicit and implicit declaration

There are two ways to declare a variable, explicitly and implicitly. The proper way to declare variables is to explicitly declare them, as was shown previously. It means you will tell Maya what type of data will be held in the variable. Implicit declaration is allowing the system to decide what type of data will be held in the variable. This can cause problems since the system doesn't always make the correct assumptions.

```
float $first = 0;
$second = 0;
$first = $first + 3.2;
//Result: 3.2//
$second = $second + 3.2;
//Result: 3//
```

When $first was declared it was explicitly declared as a float. $second was implicitly declared and since an integer value was assigned to it, Maya makes the assumption that you want an integer variable. When you try to assign a float to the integer variable the float value is truncated.

Data-type conversion

Data-type conversion lets you convert the value of one type to the value of another type. For example, when you convert a float with a value of 1.4 to an int, its value becomes 1. The table below is a summary of how each data type is converted to a different data type.

	int	float	string	vector
int ($i)	perfect	perfect	perfect	<<$i,$i,$i>>
float ($f)	truncated	perfect	perfect	<<$f,$f,$f>>
string	truncated if starts with a number, else 0	perfect if starts with number, else 0	perfect	perfect if starts with vector or floats with remaining elements 0
vector	length of vector, truncated	length of vector	3 floats separated by a space	perfect

Truncate

To truncate something means to cut it off. If you try to put a float value into an integer variable the value will be truncated, i.e. 2.3 becomes 2. Only the integer part of the value is kept. The fraction is cut off or truncated.

Operator precedence

When you start to add, subtract, multiply,or divide variables, you may encounter problems in regard to the operator precedence, especially in very complex equations. The way you typed an equation may not be read by MEL the same way. The two following lines will not generate the same results:

```
float $fVal1 = 5 + 4 / 3; // equals 6
float $fVal2 = (5 + 4) / 3; // equals 3
```

These examples were not too hard to figure out, but what about this one:

```
int $iVal = (!(4 % 5 / 0.23) <= $var[4] += 2 / 3);
```

It may be a little bit more complex to understand what MEL does (and should probably be done in separated steps). This is due to the operator precedence and you need to make sure that you know which operators are executed before the others.

The following shows the order of precedence in MEL. Operators on the same row have equal precedence. If a statement has two or more operators with the same precedence, the left-most operator is evaluated first.

Highest	( ) [ ]
	! ++ --
	* / % ^
	+ -
	< <= > >=
	== !=
	&&
	||
Lowest	= += -= *= \=

Array variables

Array variables are more complicated but they are very useful. An array variable is like a normal variable, except it can store more than one value. It's like a drawer which has dividers in it. For example, a float array can store many floats but it can still only store floats. A string array is often used to store a list of objects.

You must decide that you want a variable to be an array variable when you declare it. You do this by adding two square brackets after the name of the variable.

Example

```
float $fMyArray[];
```

In the above example, Maya knows that `$fMyArray` is an array and can hold multiple float values. The square brackets are for determining which value in the list you want to use.

Example

```
$fMyArray[0] = The first number in the array.
$fMyArray[1] = The second number in the array.
$fMyArray[2] = The third number in the array.
$fMyArray[3] = etc.
```

You can set the different values of an array this way as well. Try the following example:

Example

```
string $cool[];
$cool[0] = "Wow";
```

```
$cool[1] = "this";
$cool[2] = "is";
$cool[3] = "cool";
print $cool;
```

Each word becomes a different element in the array. Try changing the last line to only print out one element.

```
print $cool[3];
```

Using this method, you can see how you can access any element in the array in whatever order you want.

Keep in mind that an array index is zero-based. The index is the number you put in between the [ ] to specify which element in the array you are looking for. Zero-based means that you start counting at 0 instead of 1.

In the above example, you set each of the elements individually. You can also set them all at once.

Examples

```
int $intArray[5];
$intArray = {100, 1000, -70, 2, 9822};
print $intArray;


float $floatArray[4];
$floatArray = {43.3, -10.7, 0, 82.5};
print $floatArray;


string $stringArray[3];
$stringArray = {"Lord", "Flies", "cool brown fox2."};
print $stringArray;
```

Even if you specify the size of an array on declaration, it does not lock the array to that size. You will still be able to add and remove elements from it.

Array size

When accessing elements in an array, you might not know how many elements exist inside of it. A useful command is the `size` command.

Examples

- Create a random number of objects and select them all.
- Execute the following commands:

```
string $sel[] = `ls -sl`;
```

- To find out the size of the array, execute the following command:

```
size($sel);
```

This will return the number of elements in the array. Using this number, you can determine what the last element of the array is. Since the array starts at 0 the last element in the array will be accessed by using a value that is 1 less than the size of the array. This number can be used for adding new elements to an array. If the size command returns a value of 10, then you can use that value to assign the next object

```
$sel[10] = "surface1";
```

The size of the array would now be eleven with the last element being *surface1*.

Assigning the results of a command into a variable

One of the ways variables are used most often is in capturing the results of a command. When you execute a command in the Script Editor, you will notice that there is usually a result returned in the history field. The only way to keep track of these results is to assign them to variables. This is an important way to use variables since you can create an object and have the name of that object held in a variable for future use. It allows you to write scripts that are more robust since variables can be assigned at the time of execution.

If you want to get the value of an object's attribute, you should know what type of value you are capturing. This information is important so that you can determine what type of variable will be needed to hold the value, i.e. int, float, string, int array, etc. The next thing you need to know is the syntax for capturing the command. There are three different ways to capture commands: using back quotes or left-hand single quotes (`` `command` ``), using the `eval` command (`eval(command)`) or using the command with brackets (`command(arguments)`). The following example uses the back quote method:

How to capture an attribute value

```
sphere -name "mySphere";
float $fTransX;
$fTransX = `getAttr mySphere.translateX`;
```

Common ls flags
-ca -cameras
-dag -dagObjects
-g -geometry
-lt - lights
-mat -materials
-s -shapes
-tr -transforms
-sl -selection
-tex -textures
-st -showType

You will notice that there are back quotes around the `getAttr` command. This tells the system to execute the command within the back quotes first and then assign its return value to the variable.

Tip: If you are unsure of the return type of a command, you can always execute the command and watch for the return value in the history field of the Script Editor. Else, you may get an error like:
```
// Error: Line 1.19: Cannot convert data of type
string[] to string. //
```

Creating an array from a command

You should also remember that with array variables, you can cast the result of a command into them. This is probably what you will do most often. In the following example, you'll simply use this technique to print the names of all the selected objects:

- Select a bunch of objects in the interface.

- With the objects selected, enter the following script into the Script Editor.

```
string $selection[] = `ls -sl`;

print $selection;
```

When you execute the command, the selected items will be listed in the Script Editor.

The command `ls -sl` lists all the selected objects and casts them into the array variable called `$selection`. Later in this book you will take this a step further and see how you can use some of the looping functions to step through and perform operations on each object.

Tokenize

When working with variables, you often need to be able to break them up into smaller parts. For example, if you captured the name of a file texture it would include the complete path for the file, not just the name of the file.

- Open the **Windows → Rendering Editors → Hypershade**.

- In the Hypershade click on **Create → 2D Textures → File**. The texture file should appear in the Hypershade and be called *file1*.

- Double-click on *file1* to invoke the Attribute Editor and browse for an image. You can use the *snowflake* texture in the **/sourceimages/** directory or any other image.

- Enter the following in the Script Editor:

```
string $fileName = `getAttr file1.fileTextureName`;
print $fileName;
```

Your result will look something like this:

```
C:/maya/projects/MF/sourceimages/snowflake.rgb
```

Your result will be slightly different depending on your system configuration and the file used.

As you can see, the result that is returned contains the complete path for the texture file. If you only wanted to have the name of the image, you would need a method of removing it from the string being held in the $fileName variable.

tokenize works by taking a string and splitting it up by a user defined character and putting the results into a string array.

```
string $fileName = `getAttr file1.fileTextureName`;
string $afterTokenize[];
tokenize($fileName, "/", $afterTokenize);
// Result: 7 //
```

Note: If you don't define a character in the tokenize command, it will split the string where there is a space character.

Maya has taken the long string created by the getAttr command and it has split it into seven separate strings which are being held in the $afterTokenize array variable. It split the string every time it encountered a /. Any character can be used to split up a string including a space. Since it has created an array with seven elements, the last element will be at position 6 in the array (arrays start at 0). You can then print the last element in the array and that will be the name of the file.

```
print $afterTokenize[6];
```

Your result will look something like this:

```
snowflake.rgb
```

Exercises

1 Using variables

- Create several objects. Initialize an array variable that will store the names of the selected objects. Select all the objects and assign them to the array variable.

- Create a command that will print something like this:

```
The first object you picked is called "nurbsSphere1"!
```

2 Using variables in UI

- Repeat the previous exercise but this time build a window with a button and a field. When the button is pressed the statement will be placed in the field in the window.

3 Using tokenize

- Create a string variable and assign "Tokenize splits up strings by a user defined character"

- Use tokenize to split the above string into a string array.

4 Using variables in UI

- Create a window like the one that follows:

A user should be able to enter a number in the top fields, press the add button and get an answer in the bottom field.

Tip: A good workflow for building this script would be to design the window first, then create the variables you will need. After you have done that, find the way to assign values from the field to your variables and then add them into the window's functionality. The final script can be worked on in stages and is often easier to create if you do.

```
window -title "Add it up!";
columnLayout;
    text "Enter two numbers and";
    text "press add for the answer.";
    textField one;
    textField two;
    button -label "Add!" -command
```

```
        "float $one = `textField -q -text one`;\
         float $two = `textField -q -text two`;\
         float $answer = $one + $two;\
         textField -e -tx $answer answer;";
      textField answer;
    showWindow;
```

Note: In the preceding MEL commands, you will notice the back slash being used as an escape sequence. In this case, it is being used within a string. If you need to have a string broken up over multiple lines then you need to use the back slash. It tells Maya to ignore the carriage return and treat the lines as one big string. If you forget to include the back slash, you will get the following error: `//Error: Unterminated string. //`

Summary

As you move forward with more advanced expressions and scripts, you'll see how variables become a very important and powerful tool. You will be using variables and array variables to capture information generated by using different MEL commands. You'll also explore how you can use some of the looping functions to step through and perform operations on each element in these array variables.

This lesson covered the following topics:

- How to recognize different variable types

- How to declare a variable

- The naming convention

- How to assign a value to a variable

- The data-type conversion

- The operator precedence

- How to capture the result of a command in a variable

- The `tokenize` command

CHAPTER 5
Summary

6 Conditional Statements

A conditional statement, also know as the `if` statement, lets your scripts and expressions make decisions. The decision is based on a comparison that is usually between variables or attributes such as:

- If the contents of variable X are greater than the contents of variable Y, then move the sphere up.
- If the particle hits the can, knock the can over.
- If the foot touches the floor, plant it.

In this lesson, you will learn about:

- Creating simple conditional statements (`if` statements)
- Executing multiple commands with a conditional statement
- `if-else` statements
- Conditional statements in Expressions
- Logical operators
- `else-if` statements

CHAPTER 6

Simple conditional statement

To demonstrate how a conditional statement works, you will use a script to set the color of a primitive sphere based on its position.

1 Create and place a primitive sphere

- Create a sphere and rename it *ball*.

- Switch to **Smooth Shaded** mode by pressing the **5** hotkey.

- **Move** the sphere up the Y axis. Make sure it is no longer sitting at the origin (0, 0, 0).

2 Write a script using a conditional statement

- Enter the following conditional statement into the Script Editor and then execute the script.

```
float $ball = `getAttr ball.translateY`;

if ($ball > 0)
        setAttr lambert1.colorR 1;
```

Note: The *lambert1* is the name of the default shader that gets applied to all objects when they are created. The **colorR** attribute is the red value of this shader. The shader is initially gray so when the red value is changed it becomes more or less red from this base color. Hence, you get the peach to turquoise colors when this red attribute is 1 or 0, respectively.

The sphere will not change back to gray when you move it below the origin and execute the script, simply because we never reset the colorR to its original value.

This statement simply makes a variable and puts the Y position of the ball into it. Next, the if statement looks at the value for $ball and compares it to 0. If $ball is greater than 0, the next line is executed. If the statement is not true, then nothing will happen.

The comparison is always mathematical in nature. Left side is compared to right side and a decision is made as to whether the values are equal to, greater than, less than - and so on - to each other. If they are, the statement is considered to be *true* and the given command will be executed.

Here are the other operators you can use when comparing values in a conditional statement:

Symbol	True only if the left-hand side is:
<	less than the right-hand side
>	greater than the right-hand side
==	equal to the right-hand side
!=	not equal to the right-hand side
>=	greater than or equal to the right-hand side
<=	less than or equal to the right-hand side

The following shows some examples of using these operators:

Examples

```
if (-2.5 < 1) print("true\n"); // True
if (16.2 > 16.2) print("true\n"); // Nothing printed
if (-11 == -11) print("true\n"); // True
if (-11 != -11) print("true\n"); // Nothing printed
if (-11 >= -11) print("true\n"); // True
if (1 <= 0) print("true\n"); // Nothing printed
```

Note the difference between the assignment operator (=) and the equality operator (==).

The following will give you an error:

```
if(1 = 1) print "true";
// Error: Line 1.6: Syntax error //
```

But the next example will execute correctly and will change the value hold in the variable $iTmp for 1:

```
if($iTmp = 1) print "true";
true
```

Executing multiple commands

If you choose to have more than one command executed if the statement is true, you will need to enclose the commands within the brace (squiggly) brackets. This will be demonstrated using the previous example. However, this time, you will set the Red, Green, and Blue values.

1 Write a script using a conditional statement and brace brackets

- Modify the previous example like this and execute it:

```
float $ball = `getAttr ball.translateY`;
if ($ball > 0)
{
   setAttr lambert1.colorR 1;
   setAttr lambert1.colorG 0;
   setAttr lambert1.colorB 0;
}
```

Everything within the brace brackets is executed if the statement is true.

Note: It is not the indentation of the commands that makes the `if` statement execute them.

Using `if` and `else`

Often, you want the `if` statement to do something different if the statement is *false*. For instance, in this example, you may want the ball to turn red if it is above 0 but turn blue if it is below 0. Can you think of a way to do this? One way would be to use two `if` statements. Here's an example:

```
float $ball = `getAttr ball.translateY`;
if ($ball > 0)
{
   setAttr lambert1.colorR 1;
   setAttr lambert1.colorG 0;
   setAttr lambert1.colorB 0;
}
if ($ball <= 0)
{
   setAttr lambert1.colorR 0;
   setAttr lambert1.colorG 0;
   setAttr lambert1.colorB 1;
}
```

Instead of using multiple `if` statements, you can use an `if-else` statement. For example:

If condition is true, then execute A, otherwise execute B

The above `if-else` statement is like the `if` statement but if the condition is false then A is not executed but B is executed. Here's how you would write the above example:

```
float $ball = `getAttr ball.translateY`;

if ($ball > 0)
{
    setAttr lambert1.colorR 1;
    setAttr lambert1.colorG 0;
    setAttr lambert1.colorB 0;

}
else
{

    setAttr lambert1.colorR 0;
    setAttr lambert1.colorG 0;
    setAttr lambert1.colorB 1;

}
```

Execute this command with the sphere in different places. The ball's color will be either red or blue depending where it is when you execute the command.

Application: Maya Background Color Toggle

Conditional statements are a great way to help manage interface elements such as the grid, background color, resolution/film gate display and others. Commands can determine what the current state of the UI is and then change it according to the MEL statements you write.

Below is a quick MEL example you can type then copy to a shelf button or hotkey. Executing the commands toggles the color of the background between three different shades of gray.

```
float $color = `displayRGBColor -query background`;
if ($color[0] > 0.5)
        displayRGBColor background 0.15 0.15 0.15;

else
{

    if ($color[0] == 0)
        displayRGBColor background 0.675 0.675 0.675;

    else
        displayRGBColor background 0 0 0;
```

```
        }
```

Below is a similar example that can be used as a shelf button or hotkey to toggle your rendering resolution gate on or off for the perspective camera. The resolution gate shows you the portion of the camera view that will end up in your rendered image. This could be extended to work on any camera in the scene instead of just the perspective camera.

Application: Resolution gate switcher

```
if (`camera -q -displayResolution persp`)

    camera -e -displayFilmGate off
                -displayResolution off
                -overscan 1.0 persp;

else

    camera -e -displayFilmGate off
                -displayResolution on
                -overscan 1.2 persp;
```

Logical operators

You may have situations where you require a more complicated scenario to be evaluated. For instance, what if you only wanted the ball to change to red if it were above 0 but below 10? This would require a slightly more complex if statement.

> *if A and B are true, then execute C, otherwise execute D.*

Logical operators are just symbols which stand for words like *and* or *or*.

> *if ((value1 > value2) && (value1 > value3))*
>> *do this command;*

It is important to note that all the condition information has to be contained within the parentheses. That is why you have added another pair of parentheses in the above example.

These four examples are acceptable:

```
if ( val1 > val2 )
if ( (val1 > val2) && (val1 > val3) )
if ( val1 > val2 && val1 > val3 )
if ( val1 > val2 && val1 > val3 && (val2 > val3) )
```

But this will not work:

```
if ( val1 > val2 ) && ( val1 > val3 )
```

Here are the logical operators available to you:

Symbol	Means	Condition making it true
||	or	either the left side, right side, or both is true
&&	and	both left and right sides are true
!	not	right side is false (not true)

Try modifying the previous example to make the sphere red when it is between 0 and 10 in Y, but blue anywhere else. Here's what the script will look like if you use the && (*and*) operator:

```
float $ball = `getAttr ball.translateY`;

if ( ($ball > 0) && ($ball < 10) )
{
   setAttr lambert1.colorR 1;
   setAttr lambert1.colorG 0;
   setAttr lambert1.colorB 0;

}
else
{
   setAttr lambert1.colorR 0;
   setAttr lambert1.colorG 0;
   setAttr lambert1.colorB 1;

}
```

Application: Level of Detail

Level of detail usually refers to how much detail an object is drawn with based on how far it is from the camera. It is often useful to do this distance checking between objects in scripts or expressions and use it to control a variety of things (not necessarily just how much detail an object is drawn with).

For example, perhaps you want to assign shaders to objects based on their proximity to each other or the camera. The MEL commands below contain the basic information that you can use for distance checking and are set up to work with visibility by default.

In this example, Maya uses conditionals to check the object's distance from the camera. It also checks to see if the object is NURBS and if it is within a user defined distance from the camera. If it is NURBS and is greater than the user defined distance, it is hidden.

1 Create a NURBS sphere

2 Enter the following in the Script Editor:

```
//get the selection list
string $obj[] = `ls -sl`;


//get x,y,z positions of cam and object
float $camX = `getAttr persp.tx`;
float $camY = `getAttr persp.ty`;
float $camZ = `getAttr persp.tz`;
float $objX = `getAttr ($obj + ".tx")`;
float $objY = `getAttr ($obj + ".ty")`;
float $objZ = `getAttr ($obj + ".tz")`;


//establish vectors from the above info
vector $camVec = <<$camX, $camY, $camZ>>;
vector $objVec = <<$objX, $objY, $objZ>>;


//subtract the camera and the object position and
//take the magnitude of the resulting vector. This
//gives the distance from the object to the camera
//as a float value.
float $dist = mag($camVec - $objVec);


//Find the shape node of the selected object
//so you can test it to find out if it is a NURBS
//surface or not.
string $shapeNode[] = `listRelatives $obj[0]`;
string $nodeType = `nodeType $shapeNode[0]`;
int $vis = `getAttr ($obj[0] + ".visibility")`;
int $threshold = 20;


//If the object is greater than the threshold (20
//units) from the camera AND is a nurbsSurface AND it
//is currently visible, then hide it
if (($dist > $threshold) && ($nodeType ==
                        "nurbsSurface") && ($vis))
{
    setAttr ($obj[0] + ".visibility") 0;
```

```
          print ($obj[0] + " is " + $dist +
                " units from the camera and WAS HIDDEN");
      }
      else
      {
          setAttr ($obj[0] + ".visibility") 1;
          print ($obj[0] + " NOT HIDDEN, it is " + $dist +
                " units from the camera and is of type: " +
                $nodeType);
      }
```

3 Dolly the camera far and near to ball and re-execute

- Move the camera then execute the commands again and watch the output to the Script Editor for feedback.

Note: Maya has level of detail visibility sets built in. See **Edit** -> **Level of Detail**. The above example shows you the basic idea of how that was implemented so that you can expand the applications.

Review the `if-else` statement

Conditional statements let you execute a statement only if the test condition is true. This test condition must be enclosed in parentheses. The `if` conditional statement has the following format:

```
      if (test condition)
          statement;
```

Only if test condition is true, is the statement executed. If the test condition is false, then the statement is not executed. The following shows an example of using an `if` statement:

```
      if (true)
          print("Wow, that's interesting!\n");
```

The `else` statement works only with the `if` conditional statement. It has the following format:

```
      if (test condition)
          statement1;
      else
          statement2;
```

If test condition is true, statement1 executes, otherwise statement2 executes. The statement1 and statement2 can be any valid commands as the following examples illustrate:

```
if ($tmp > 2)
    print("Bigger than 2.\n");
else
    print("Less or equal to 2.\n");
```

else-if statement

In addition to the `if` and `if-else` statements, you can also use an `else-if` statement to test for a new condition if the first condition is false. Try experimenting with it. It has the following format:

```
if (test condition1)
    statement1;
else if (test condition2)
    statement2;
else
    statement3;
```

If test condition1 is true, statement1 executes. Otherwise, if test condition2 is true, statement2 executes. If neither test condition is true, statement3 will be executed.

Note: If two or more conditions are true, MEL executes the first one encountered.

Exercises

1 Using `if`

- Write a command that will test if a window exists, and if it does, delete it.

2 Using `if-else`

- Open the file *06.TrainCrossing.ma*.
- Create a condition statement that will test the train's position and raise or lower the crossing gate, using only one `if-else`.

3 Using `else-if`

- Continue using the scene file *06.TrainCrossing.ma*.

- Create a condition statement that will test the train's position and raise or lower the crossing gate, using only one `else-if`.

4 Using conditionals in a window

- Continue using the scene file *06.TrainCrossing.ma*.

- Modify exercise three to display the information in a window. Use radio buttons to represent the three possible positions of the gate and a button to refresh the values.

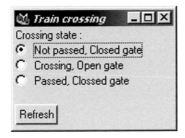

5 Other conditional statements

- Look in the on-line documentation for other conditional statements such as the `switch` statement and the `?:` operator.

Summary

Through the use of conditional statements and logical operators, you give your commands the power to make decisions based on the data provided by the user.

7 Looping Statements

Loop statements are designed to repeatedly execute statements while a certain test condition is true. All the lights in a scene could be selected, and a loop could be used to change the color of each light in turn. If you were to write the commands to do this, you could write one command for each light but this would be very rigid. What would happen if the user of the script added a light or removed one? By using a loop, you could avoid situations such as this.

In this lesson, you will learn about the following loop statements:

- `for`
- `for in`

While learning loops, the following functions will also be introduced:

- `sin`
- `cos`
- `rand`
- `sphrand`

CHAPTER 7

FOR STATEMENT

A for statement is useful when you want to do something a certain number of times. This is called a *loop*. The for loop has the following format:

```
for (start value; end value; increment value)
    statement;
```

for loops use a variable to keep track of how many times the statement has repeated. In the next few examples, you will refer to this variable as $i. $i will start at 0 and the statement will loop until $i equals 20.

Just like the if statement, you need brace brackets in order to execute more than one line.

Note: If you execute a loop that would never end, there is no way of stopping its execution. You would need to force the ending of the Maya session.

Simple for statement

You will see here how to create a for loop that tells the statement to repeat itself 20 times.

1 Typing your first loop statement

- Enter the following in the Script Editor, then execute it:

```
for ($i = 0; $i < 20; $i = $i + 1)
{
    print ($i + " ");
}
print " Done\n";
```

The statement print ($i + " "), loops 20 times. Each time, $i increases by 1 until $i is no longer less than 20. A shortcut can be used to increase the value of $i each time.

Instead of writing:

```
$i = $i + 1
```

You can write:

```
$i++
```

or

```
$i += 1
```

These are shortcuts to add 1 to the value of $i. Often in scripting you will want to assign a variable the value of itself plus or minus some other value. The shortcut operations give you a quick and simple way to do this.

The following table shows all of the shortcuts which are available to you and how they are used.

Shortcut Syntax	Expanded Syntax
`variable += value;`	`variable = variable + value;`
`variable -= value;`	`variable = variable - value;`
`variable *= value;`	`variable = variable * value;`
`variable /= value;`	`variable = variable / value;`
`variable++;`	`variable = variable + 1;`
`variable--;`	`variable = variable - 1;`

Take the first example a bit further. Try using a `for` loop to create 20 spheres in a row.

2 Create a `for` loop to create 20 spheres in a row

- Execute the following commands in the Script Editor:

```
for ($i = 0; $i < 20; $i++)
{
   sphere -pivot 0 $i 0;
}
```

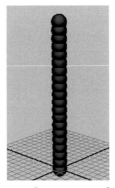

Spheres created one on top of each other

First, you begin a `for` loop — the first section (`$i = 0;`) establishes the start value of the `for` loop. `$i` is given a start value of 0 in this example. The second section (`$i < 20;`) determines when the loop will end or the number of iterations the loop will go through. The third section (`$i++`) tells us how we are going to get from the start value to the end value. The double plus sign means increment by 1. This `for` loop will start at 0, check to see if the condition is true, execute the commands in the curly brackets and then increment by 1. It then starts at the condition (`$i < 20;`) again and checks to see if it is true. If it is true then the loop continues until the value of 20 is reached and the condition is no longer true.

The command you are executing in this loop is the `sphere` command. It is executed 20 times (once for every time the statement loops). To prevent all 20 spheres from appearing in exactly the same place, the Y position of the sphere equal to `$i`. Since `$i` is increasing by 1 every time, the position of the new sphere increases by 1 every time as well.

`for` statements with Maya's math functions

Maya has built-in math functions which allow you to process math operations with greater ease. Here are some slightly more complex examples using `for` loops and Maya's math functions.

These math functions can be used for many things, including creating randomness, adding noise, performing mathematical operations like sine or cosine and to print information in the Script Editor.

You can explore all of the available math functions through the on-line docs.

Here are a few loop examples:

1 `for` loop with `sphrand`

- Type the following commands in the Script Editor. It will place spheres randomly within a specified radius:

```
vector $vNum;

for ($i = 0; $i < 20; $i++)
{
    $vNum = sphrand(10);
    sphere -pivot ($vNum.x) ($vNum.y) ($vNum.z);
}
```

The `rand` function

The `rand` function will return a random number.

If one number is specified, the return value will be between 0 and that number:

```
rand (5);
// Result: 3.73450 //
```

If two numbers are specified, the return value will be in between:

```
rand (5,10);
// Result: 7.72617 //
```

The `sphrand` function

The `sphrand` function will return a random vector (3 values) within a sphere of the specified radius.

```
sphrand (1);
// Result:
<<-0.02028899,
0.5405627,
0.5669539>>  //
```

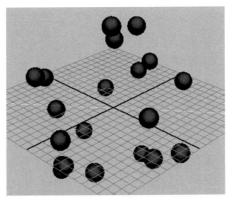

Spheres created randomly

The seed command allows you to make your random numbers less random. If you want to have the same randomness every time you execute a rand function, you can give it a seed value.

```
seed 2;
rand 5;
```

This time, you declared a vector variable (an empty drawer for storing 3 floats), called $rand, before entering the for loop. Next, you entered the loop and again created 20 spheres. This time, however, you used a simple function called sphrand to assign a new value to $rand every time and then used that value to place the sphere.

If you execute the above example you will always get the same result. If you create a script that positions objects in a scene, you won't want them to be placed in different positions each time. Using the seed value, you can make sure that the objects are always in the same position.

Tip: You can access the individual values of a vector variable by using the .x, .y, and .z extensions. For example, if you wanted just the first value from this variable, $rgb = <<1,0,0>>, you could simply ask for $rgb.x. $rgb.x will be equal to 1.

---

2 for loop with sin and cos

- The following will create a helix shape with spheres:

```
for ($i = 0; $i < 20; $i++)
{
    float $fSin = sin($i);
    float $fCos = cos($i);
    sphere -p $fSin $i $fCos;
}
```

Standard trigonometric functions like sin and cos are available.

The function is entered followed by the number to process:

```
sin (45);
// Result: 0.8509 //
```

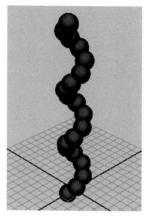

Spheres created in helix

3 Another `for` loop with `sin` and `cos`

- This will create a spiral with spheres:

```
for ($i = 0; $i < 100; $i++)
{
    float $fSin = sin($i) *$i/4;
    float $fCos = cos($i) *$i/4;
    sphere -p $fCos 0 $fSin;
}
```

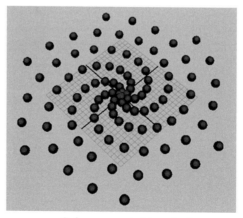

Spheres created in spiral

4 `for` loop with modeling commands

- These commands will create a spring like surface:

```
circle;

move 4 0 0;

move 0 0 0 nurbsCircle1.rotatePivot;

for ($i = 0; $i < 60; $i++)

{

    duplicate;

    rotate -r 0 30 0;

    move -r 0 0.3 0;

}

select -all;

loft;
```

A spring surface

5 More `for` loop with modeling commands

- Open *07.Hoops_Start.ma*.

- Run these MEL commands in the Script Editor:

```
select -clear;

select -hi -all;

select -tgl "nurbsCircleShape1";

string $curves[] = `ls -sl -type "nurbsCurve"`;

for ($i = 0; $i < `size($curves)`; $i++)

{

    extrude -ch true -rn false -po 0 -et 2 -ucp 1
            -fpt 1 -upn 1 -rotation 0 -scale 1
            -rsp 1 "nurbsCircle1" $curves[$i];
```

```
}
select -clear;
```

The above commands clear the selection list then get a list of all the NURBS curves in the scene. An extrusion is built for each of the net curves using *nurbsCircle1* as the profile curve and each net curve as the path curve. For more information about the flags used on the extrude command, type `help extrude;` in the Script Editor or check the online MEL documentation. The file *07.Hoops_Finish.ma* is a finished version.

The geometry created with MEL commands

Infinite Loops

Any time you are creating loops in Maya, you should be careful that your conditions do not always evaluate as *true*. If they do, Maya will never exit the loop and you will have to exit the software to regain control.

Below is an example of an **infinite loop** (don't execute these commands!)

```
for ($i = 0; $i >= 0; $i++)
    print $i;
```

In the above case, $i will *always* be greater than or equal to 0 so the loop will never exit.

Some people put a checking statement or routine inside the loop for the existence of a file on the hard drive. If that file exists then the condition can be made false, causing the loop to exit.

```
for(;;)
{
   if(`filetest -f "c:/break.mel"`)
      break;
}
```

However, this check would need to exist in every problematic loop, so it is better to just watch your conditions closely before testing your loops.

Break and continue statements

The `break` statement exits a loop immediately. It is usually preceded by an `if` statement that will decide if it needs to exit the loop.

The `continue` statement works just like the `break` command, but instead of breaking the loop, it will force the next iteration of the loop to occur, skipping any remaining statements in the loop.

Variable scope

When dealing with variables and different command structures you need to be aware of variable scope. This is defined as what area of the command structure knows about the variable. If a variable is created within a `for` loop it only exists within that `for` loop. The body of the loop is the scope of the variable. We would say that this variable is a Local variable to this loop. Once the `for` loop ends the variable no longer exists. The same thing can be said for `if` statements. Following is an example:

```
for ($a = 1; $a < 10; $a++)
{
   print ($a + "\n");
   int $b = 25;
   print ($b + "\n");
}
print ($a + "\n");
print ($b + "\n");
```

On execution, this returns:

```
// Error: print ($b + "\n"); //
// Error: "$b" is an undeclared variable. //
```

The error comes from the `print` statement that is outside of the `for` loop. $b was declared inside of the `for` loop so it is known only to the `for` loop. If $b was needed to be accessed outside the loop, the example should be rewritten as:

```
int $b;
for ($a = 1; $a < 10; $a++)
{
    print ($a + "\n");
    $b = 25;
    print ($b + "\n");
}
print ($a + "\n");
print ($b + "\n");
```

Try to keep this in mind when creating variables.

Tip: { } are the scope characters. That is why we usually add an indentation to the commands between them. It's a reminder that variables declared there are local to this scope. You could also use the scope characters without being preceded by a `for` or an `if` statement.

---

for-in **statement**

The `for-in` loop is very useful. It is a specialized version of the `for` loop which allows you to easily deal with arrays. Often you might want to step through all the elements of an array. A `for` loop could do this but it would require a counter to retain the array index. For example, you'd have to find out how many items are in the array and then step through them one at a time.

The `for-in` loop simplifies this process by only requiring an element variable. An element variable is just a variable which the `for-in` loop will use to step through an array. The `for-in` loop has the following format:

```
for (element in array)
    statement;
```

The statement will loop once for every element in the array. So, for example, if there were 10 items in the array, the statement would loop 10 times.

The following shows a very common way of using the `for-in` loop:

1 Create several spheres

2 Execute a series of MEL commands using the for-in loop

- **Select** all the spheres.
- Type the following command in the Script Editor:

```
string $sel[] = `ls -sl`;

string $current;

for ($current in $sel)

{

    print("The current item is " + $current + "\n");

}

print "No more items.";
```

The following will be printed in the Script Editor when you execute the preceding commands:

```
The current item is nurbsSphere1
The current item is nurbsSphere2
The current item is nurbsSphere3
No more items.
```

As this `for` loop is entered the first element in the array is assigned to the variable `$current`. After all the commands in the curly brackets are executed, Maya goes back to the top of the `for` loop. The next element in the array is then assigned to the variable `$current`. The `for` loop continues until there are no more elements in the array. This technique can be very useful for creating simple, time saving scripts and tools.

For example, modify the above example to automatically rename all the selected objects to *ball* instead of *nurbsSphere*.

```
string $sel[] = `ls -sl`;

string $current;

for ($current in $sel)

{

    rename $current "ball#";

}
```

All the selected items are put into, or cast into, the array variable `$sel`. Then, the `for-in` loop steps through all the items in the array and renames each one.

Tip: By using the # sign as part of the name, the rename command knows to just add a number to the end of the name if the name already exists. This prevents annoying warnings when you are renaming several objects to the same name.

Nested Control Structures

In the following example, you will use two `for-in` loops to capture different character poses which you can add to your shelf. You will use one loop to go through a list of selected objects, then a second loop to go through all of the keyable attributes for each of the selected objects.

1 Open an existing file

- Open the file *07.Legs.ma*.

2 Select all the objects for your pose buttons

3 Enter the following script into the Script Editor:

You do not have to enter the comment lines, they are simply there to help explain how the script is working.

```
//Go through the selected objects one at a time
for ($item in `ls -sl`)
{
    string $attribute;   //the attribute in the list
    float $value;        //the attribute's value


    //Go through the keyable attributes of this object
    //one at a time
    for ($attribute in `listAttr -k $item `)
    {
        //Get the current value
        $value = `getAttr ($item + "." + $attribute )`;
        //Create a setAttr command
        print ("setAttr " + $item + "." + $attribute +
                        " " + $value + ";\n");

    }
}
```

4 Put this script into the shelf

- Highlight the script you just typed and with **LMB** drag onto shelf.

- **Label** this new button *getAttr*.

With this in the shelf, you can execute it easily by pressing the shelf button.

5 Select the following from the Outliner:

> *back_root*
>
> *left_ankleLocator*
>
> *right_ankleLocator*

6 Press the getAttr button in shelf

- Once you execute the script, all of the `setAttr` for the current positions will be printed into the history field of the Script Editor.

7 Create a new button for the pose

- Dragging the lines to the shelf will create a pose button for easily animating a character.

Try making several different poses using the output from this script and the character provided in the *07.Legs.ma* file.

Creating an AutoUI

In this example, you will use two `for-in` loops to go through a list of selected objects and find out the keyable attributes on each object. With this information, you will then build a window with sliders and keyframe buttons to control the objects in your scene.

1 Enter the following script into the Script Editor:

```
window -title "Auto UI";

gridLayout -numberOfColumns 2 -cellWidth 400;

text -l "Keyable Attributes";

text -l "";


for ($current in `ls -sl`)
{
    separator -w 400 -style "out";

    text -l "";

    text -l $current;

    text -l "";


    for ($Attr in `listAttr -keyable $current`)
    {
        attrFieldSliderGrp -min -40 -max 40
```

Some gridLayout flags

-ch cellHeight

-cw cellWidth

-cwh cellWidthHeight

-nc numberOfColumns

-nr numberOfRows

-nrc

numberOfRowsColumns

```
            -at ($current + "." + $Attr);
        button -l "KeyFrame" -w 100
            -c ("setKeyframe " + $current + "." + $Attr);
    }
}
showWindow;
```

2 Select an object or objects and execute the script

If you have selected too many objects so you cannot see the items at the bottom of the list, try looking up a `scrollLayout` in the MEL documentation and see if you can add scroll bars to the window.

Exercises

1 Using `for` loops

- Create a script that will place a specified number of trees randomly on the ground. A cone can be used to represent a tree.

2 Using `for-in` loops

- Write a script that will create a window that controls the intensity of all the lights in the scene, no matter how many there are.

3 Creating a vertical list

- The `listAttr` command returns all the attributes on a given object. Create a script that builds a window and lists all the attributes in the window vertically.

4 Creating a forest

- Modify the first exercise so that it has a window to control it. The user should be able to place different trees with the window.

5 Other loop statements

- Look in the on-line documentation for other loop statements such as the `while` and `do-while` statements.

Summary

Looping statements allow you to do multiple iterations of a task while a certain test condition is true. Looping offers you great control and power when you write your scripts. The `for` and `for-in` loops have been covered in this section.

8 Expressions

This lesson describes some of the basic concepts of Maya expressions. You'll see several simple examples that show how using expressions can simplify and automate components of your scene. In this lesson, you will learn about:

- Expressions

- Predefined `time` and `frame` variables

- Expression syntax

    Syntax shortcuts

    Naming abbreviations

- More Sine and Cosine functions

- More Random functions

- Curve functions

    `Linstep`

    `Smoothstep`

- Using time delayed expressions and "control" objects

CHAPTER 8

INTRODUCTION TO EXPRESSIONS

In this lesson, you will learn some basic expression writing skills. Expressions are an alternative to keyframing and, in some cases, are the only way to get the complex motion you are trying to achieve. Expressions are evaluated on every frame that an animation plays, similar to keyframes.

Expressions are often as simple as a few words or lines—you don't need to be a mathematician or programmer to learn how to use them.

Expressions can be added to any keyable object attribute. Dynamic expressions that control *per particle* or *per object* attributes are the most commonly used, but expressions can be used in modeling, animating, and rendering to control a number of aspects of a scene.

Expressions don't need to be attached to specific attributes. You can have one expression that contains all your MEL commands for the scene. This can be helpful in organizing your expressions since you will be able to access all of them at the same time.

Note: You cannot apply an expression to an attribute that has an input connection, such as keys, set driven keys, constraints, or connections.

In this lesson, you will go through the different steps to create various parts of the scene and learn how to integrate the same type of expressions into your workflow.

Expression Editor

The Expression Editor is the window you will be using to add expressions to objects in your scene. It is located under **Window → Animation Editors → Expression Editor...** or through the **Ctrl + e** hotkey.

The parts of the Editor you will be using are the **Select Filter**, **Expression Name**, the **Selection** frame, and the **Expression** text field.

Tip: You can also edit expressions with a text editor, such as *jot*, or *wordpad* by selecting the text editor from the **Editor** pull-down menu above the **Expression** text field. You can then double-click on an expression name or create a new expression to automatically invoke the text editor. (Note that it does not keep a file on your drive.)

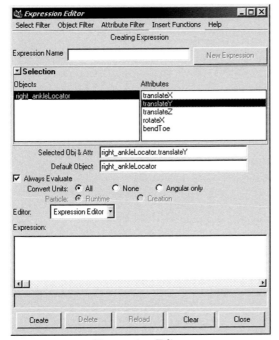

Expression Editor

Simple expressions

There are two predefined variables in all expressions that Maya maintains as an animation plays. These variables are provided by Maya because they are so frequently used by expression writers. These variables are `time` and `frame`, both of which are floating point values and give an indicator of where the current scene evaluation is. Your expressions can read, but not set, the value of `time` and `frame`.

Note: The `time` and `frame` variables are not user variables like `$time` and `$frame`.

Predefined time and frame variables

The `frame` variable gives the current frame of the scene evaluation. For example, if the animation is on the thirty-seventh frame of the scene, the `frame` variable would be equal to 37.

The `time` variable gives the current time of the scene evaluation in the current time units. The current time units are most often seconds.

```
time = frame / frameRate
```

For example, if the frame rate is twenty-four frames per second and the animation is at frame 1, the elapsed time is 1 divided by 24, or 0.0417. At frame 10, the elapsed time is 10 divided by 24 or 0.4166.

Frame 24 f/s	Time (seconds)
0	0
1	0.0417
2	0.0833
5	0.1250
50	2.0833
240	10.0

The following example shows how you use these predefined variables:

Using `frame` in an expression

You will now write a script that positions a sphere based on the current frame value. The sphere will move one unit for every frame during play back.

1 Create a sphere

- Select **Create** → **NURBS Primitives** → **Sphere**.
- Rename the sphere *frameSphere*.

2 Open the Expression Editor

- Select **Window** → **Animation Editors**→ **Expression Editor**.

3 Enter an expression

- In the **Expression Name** field enter *frameExpression*.
- In the **Expression** text field enter the following expression:

```
frameSphere.translateX = frame;
```

- Press the **Create** button.

  If there is a problem with the expression, Maya will give you an error and the expression will not be entered.

4 Test the results

- Playback the scene.

Using `time` in an expression

You will now write a similar expression that links the position of a sphere to time. The sphere will move one unit for every second. By default, Maya is set at 24 frames per second, so the sphere will move one unit for every twenty-four frames.

1 Create a new sphere

- Select **Create** → **NURBS Primitives** → **Sphere**.

- Rename the sphere *timeSphere*.

2 Open the Expression Editor

- Select **Window** → **Animation Editors** → **Expression Editor**.

3 Enter an expression

- In the **Expression Name** field enter *timeExpression*.

- In the **Expression** text field enter the following expression:

```
timeSphere.translateX = time;
```

- Press the **Create** button at the lower left corner of the window.

- If there is a problem with the expression this is when Maya will give you an error and the expression will not be entered.

4 Test the results

- Playback the scene.

  The two spheres will be moving at different speeds. The *timeSphere* should be moving twenty-four times slower than the *frameSphere*.

Editing expressions

This shows how to edit an expression to redefine how it works, using the Expression Editor.

1 View the frameExpression in the Expression Editor

- Select **Window** → **Animation Editors** → **Expression Editor**.

- Select **Select Filter** → **By Expression Name**.

  This will list all of the expressions in the scene in the **Expressions** text field.

- Select *frameExpression*.

2 Edit the Expression

- Change the expression to the following:

  ```
  frameSphere.translateX = (frame / 2) + 1;
  ```

- Press the **Edit** button in the lower left corner of the window.

  The **Edit** button used to be labeled **Create** in the previous example when the expression was first entered.

3 Test the results

- Playback the scene.

Tip: Be careful when entering expressions. If the expression is complex, it is a good idea to drag a copy to the Script Editor or shelf, or save it in a separate text file on your disk.

Adding to expressions

An expression can be multiple lines and can control multiple attributes on an object or objects. Here you'll add onto the *timeExpression*.

1 View the frameExpression in the Expression Editor

- Select **Window** → **Animation Editors** → **Expression Editor**.

- Select **Filter** → **By Expression Name**.

- Select *timeExpression*.

- Add the following lines to the end of the existing expression:

  ```
  timeSphere.translateZ = time - 1;

  timeSphere.scaleY = time * 10;

  timeSphere.rotateY = time * 20;
  ```

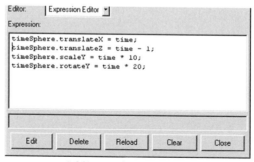

Adding to the expression

- Press the **Edit** button.

2 Test the results

- Playback the scene.

  Now the sphere moves along two axes while rotating and scaling. The expression is controlling all of these attributes using `time`.

EXPRESSION SYNTAX

To create expressions, you are essentially creating MEL commands that are embedded into your Maya file. Following are some of the syntax conventions that you may use in your expressions:

Comment markers

A comment marker lets you put notes in an expression just like in scripts. These notes don't get evaluated, but they make it easy for you or another person to find out what an expression, or certain part of an expression, is doing. To create a comment, enter two forward slashes //, then enter the comment. You can also use the /* */ couple for longer comments.

Example:

```
// Get a list of the selected objects
string $list[] = `ls -sl`;
/*
print $list;
*/
```

Anything following on the same line as the // comment marker and anything between the /* */ couple, is ignored by Maya. Any other following uncommented line(s) of the expression is executed.

Comment markers can also be used to turn off all or parts of an expression so it is not evaluated. You may want to explore another option or see how the scene works without the expression. You may temporarily disable it by commenting out that line(s).

`sin` and `cos` functions

`sin`

This function returns the sin of an angle specified in radians. With a steadily increasing or decreasing argument, the `sin` function returns a steadily increasing and decreasing value between -1 and 1. This is useful for creating rhythmic, oscillating changes in attribute values.

Syntax:

```
sin(number);
```

Example:

You could use the `sin` function to manipulate:

- an object's translate attributes to create snake-like motion
- a body's scale attributes to create a breathing cycle
- a particle object's opacity or color attributes to cycle a color or opacity pattern

---

Tip: When working with `sin` and `cos` in expressions there are two values that can be modified to change the amplitude or the frequency of the curve. To understand how to change the amplitude or frequency of an expression with `sin`, use this syntax:

```
amplitude * sin( frequency * value )
```

The following are motion paths of a ball with the given expression applied to its transforms:

```
ball.tx = time;
ball.ty = sin(time);
```

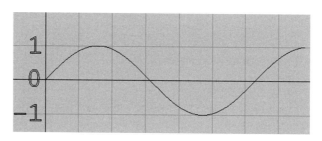

```
ball.tx = time;
ball.ty = sin(time) * 2;
```

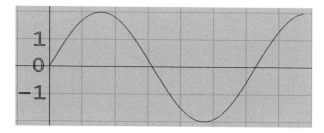

```
ball.tx = time;
ball.ty = sin(time * 2);
```

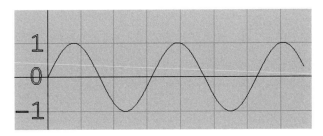

```
ball.tx = time;
ball.ty = sin(time * 5);
```

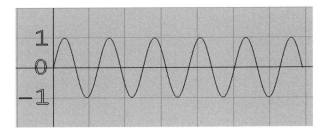

cos

Returns the cosine of an angle specified in radians. The cosine ratio is a value between 1 and -1. The basic difference between `sin` and `cos` is an offset on the starting position. With a steadily increasing or decreasing argument, the `cos` function returns steadily increasing and decreasing value between 1 and -1.

Syntax:

```
cos(number);
```

The following are motion paths of a ball with the given expression applied to its transforms.

```
ball.tx = time;
ball.ty = cos(time);
```

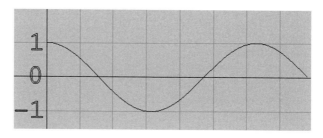

```
ball.tx = time;
ball.ty = cos(time) * 2;
```

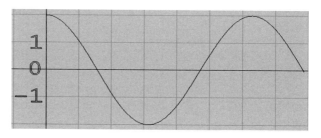

```
ball.tx = time;
ball.ty = cos(time / 2);
```

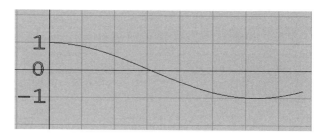

Simple Sine and Cosine expressions

Sine example:

1 Open a new scene

- Select **File** → **New Scene**.

2 Create a sphere

- Select **Create** → **NURBS Primitives** → **Sphere**.
- Rename the sphere *sinBall*.

3 Create the following expression

- Select **Window** → **Animation Editors** → **Expression Editor**.
- Enter the following in the **Expression** text field:

```
sinBall.tx = time;
sinBall.ty = sin(time);
```

- Click on the **Create** button.

4 Test the results

- Playback the scene.

Cosine example:

5 Add another sphere to the scene

- Select **Create** → **NURBS Primitives** → **Sphere**.
- Rename the sphere *cosBall*.

6 Create the following expression

- Click on **New Expression** at the top of the Expression Editor.
- Enter the following in the **Expression** text field:

```
cosBall.tx = time;
cosBall.ty = sin(time);
```

- Click on the **Create** button.

7 Test the results

- Playback the scene.

  You will see that the two balls are oscillating with an offset relative to each other.

Exercise: more `sin` and `cos` expressions

Try some different configurations of the `sin` and `cos` functions, to effect the amplitude and frequency of the movement.

Examples:

```
sinBall.tx = time;
sinBall.ty = sin(frame);


cosBall.tx = time;
cosBall.ty = sin(time / 10);
```

```
cosBall.tx = cos(time);
cosBall.ty = sin(time);

sinBall.tx = cos(frame);
sinBall.ty = sin(time);
```

Random functions

In this exercise, you will learn a useful MEL function called `rand` that generates random numbers for you. This function returns a random floating point number within a range of your choice. You could use this function to control:

- the random placement of trees on a landscape
- different radius values on individual particles
- the flickering of a light

Examples:

The following syntax will return a random float number between 0 and 10:

```
rand(10);
```

In this example, a float number between 5 and 20 will be returned:

```
rand(5, 20);
```

The following are examples of motion paths of a ball with the given expression applied to its transforms:

```
ball.tx = time;
ball.ty = rand(1);
```

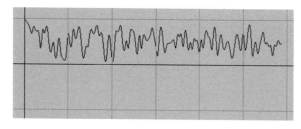

```
ball.tx = time;
ball.ty = rand(-1, 1);
```

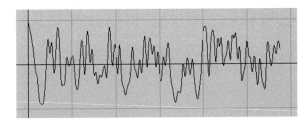

```
ball.tx = time;
ball.ty = rand(time);
```

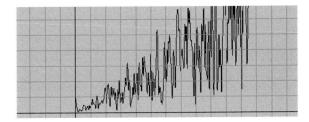

Jitter expression

This expression uses the rand function to vary the position of a sphere.

1 Create a new scene

2 Create and rename a sphere

- Select **Create** → **NURBS Primitives** → **Sphere**.

- Rename the sphere *jitter*.

3 Create a new expression

- Open the Expression Editor.

- Name the new expression *jitterExpression*.

- Enter the following into the **Expresssion** text field:

```
float $fAmount = 3;
jitter.translateX = rand($fAmount);
jitter.translateY = rand($fAmount);
jitter.translateZ = rand($fAmount);
```

- Press the **Create** button.

4 Test the results

- Playback the scene.

Exercise: more `rand` expressions

Now try the same using the following expressions:

```
float $fMin = 3;
float $fMax = 4;
jitter.translateX = rand($fMin, $fMax);
jitter.translateY = rand($fMin, $fMax);
jitter.translateZ = rand($fMin, $fMax);


float $fMin = time;
float $fMax = frame;
jitter.translateX = rand($fMin, $fMax);
jitter.translateY = rand($fMin, $fMax);
jitter.translateZ = rand($fMin, $fMax);
```

Note: The `$fMin` and `$fMax` variables are used here to simplify the expression. By using the variables, if the min and max values needed to be changed, they would only have to be changed once each, as opposed to three times each if not using them.

The Noise function

You may have noticed that the motion produced by the `rand` function is very jittery and jumpy. Another pseudo-random generator in Maya called `noise` produces a much smoother random stream of numbers. The syntax is as follows:

```
amplitude * noise (a changing value * freq)
```

For example, create a sphere, rename it *ball* and add the expression:

```
ball.ty = 5 * noise (frame/10);
```

This produces a more fluid random motion along the Y axis of the sphere than if `rand` were to be used.

In general, `rand` is better for picking things like random particle lifespans or random values that do not change. Noise generally works better when a random number stream is needed.

| **Tip:** | rand and noise both return float values. Their respective vector random generators are sphrand (spheric random) and dnoise (dimensional noise). |

Function test script

The following script was written to see the resulting curve of different functions in Maya. You may find it useful to try some different values and see the results achieved.

1 Create a new scene

- Select **File** → **New Scene**.

- Source the functionTest.mel script from your script directory by either typing source functionTest or by dragging the file over the Maya interface.

| **Note:** | If you have the installed the MEL Fundamentals *maya* folder, it should be sourced automatically. |

2 Launching the script

- Type the command to launch the script.

functionTest

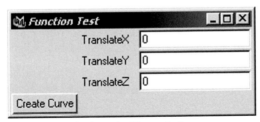

The functionTest window

3 Typing the parameters for the functionTest script

- Enter the following into the appropriate fields:

TranslateX : time

TranslateY : sin(time)

TranslateZ : 0

Note:	Make sure your timeline is set to at least 300 frames.

4 Execute the script

- Press the **Create Curve** button.

Entering new values in the text fields and pressing the Create Curve button again creates another curve which makes it very easy to see the differences.

Tip:	You can also see the resulting function curve produced by an expression in the Graph Editor. Select the object containing the expression and choose **View → Show Results** from within the Graph Editor. The resulting curve is not editable but will quickly update if you change the expresssion.

CURVE FUNCTIONS

The curve (or step) functions let you make smooth, incrementing transitions between values. The functions you will be focusing on will be `linstep` and `smoothstep`.

linstep

The `linstep` function returns a value from 0 to 1 that represents a parameter's proportional distance between a minimum and maximum value with a *linear* interpolation.

You could use `linstep` to control:

- the movement of an object within a given frame range.

- the opacity of particles to achieve a fade to black look rather than a sudden jump on and off (also called *puffing*).

- the color of a shader and the transition from one to another.

Syntax:

```
linstep(start, end, parameter);
```

`start` and `end` specify the minimum and maximum values.

`parameter` is the value you want to use to generate the proportional number.

If `parameter` is less than start, `linstep` returns 0.

If `parameter` is greater than end, `linstep` returns 1.

Example:

```
ball.tx = linstep(5, 25, frame);
```

The following example shows the values of `ball.tx`:

Frame	ball.tx
< 5	0
6	0.05
7	0.1
8	0.15
9	0.2
10	0.25
12	0.35
15	0.5
20	0.75
24	0.95
> 25	1

These are examples of motion paths of a ball with the given expression applied to its transforms:

```
ball.tx = time;
ball.ty = linstep(0, 25, frame);
```

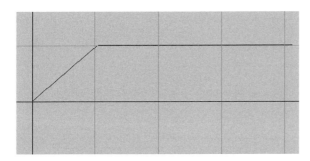

```
ball.tx = time;
ball.ty = linstep(20, 40, frame);
```

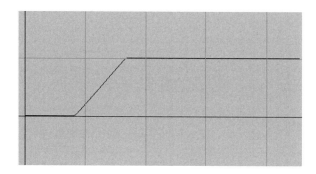

`smoothstep`

The `smoothstep` function is essentially the same as `linstep` except the result is a gradual start and end of a curve from 0 to 1.

Syntax:

```
smoothstep(start, end, parameter);
```

Example:

```
ball.tx = smoothstep( 5, 25, frame );
```

Frame	ball.tx
< 5	0
6	.007
7	.028
8	.060
9	.104
10	.156
12	.282
15	.5
20	.844
24	.993
> 25	1

The following are examples of motion paths of a ball with the given expression applied to its transforms:

```
ball.tx = time;

ball.ty = smoothstep( 0, 25, frame );
```

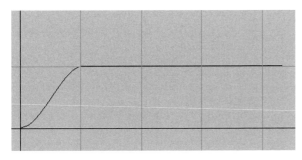

```
ball.tx = time;
ball.ty = 1 - smoothstep( 5, 10, (frame / 4) );
```

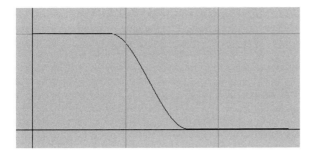

Usage Example

The most common uses for linstep and smoothstep are controlling dynamic attributes.

Example:

```
particle.opacityPP = 1 - linstep(0, lifespan, age);
```

or

```
particle.opacityPP = 1 - smoothstep(0, lifespan,
                                    age);
```

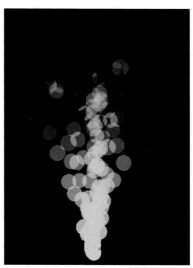

Particles using a step expression for transparency

PARTICLE EXPRESSIONS

Particle expressions are more complex than other types of expressions. For example, you can write an expression to control all particles in an object the same way or you can control each particle differently. Also, executing particle expressions differs from other types of expressions. To become proficient with such expressions takes more study than for other expressions, but the resulting effects are often worth the effort. This lesson guides you through some basics of working with particle expressions.

There are two types of particle expressions: `creation` and `runtime`. A `creation` expression is evaluated for each particle on the first frame of a particle's life. The `runtime` expression is evaluated once per frame for each particle on every frame of a particle's life.

Example: `linstep` expression

In this example you will create a particle emitter and add creation and runtime expressions to control the lifespan and radius of the particles. The particles will emit and grow larger and eventually fade out as they die.

1 Start a new scene

2 Create an Emitter

- Particles → Create Emitter.

- Name the emitter *smokeSource.*
- Set its attributes like the following:

  EmitterType to **Directional**

  Rate to **50**

  Direction X to **0**

  Direction Y to **1**

  Direction Z to **0**

  Spread to **0.25**

  Speed to **2**

- Name the particles *smokePart.*

3 Add a radiusPP to smokePart

- Add a *radiusPP* (radius per particle) using MEL.

```
addAttr -ln "radiusPP" -dt doubleArray
                           smokePartShape;
```

4 Change the particle type

- **Select** the particles and open the Attribute Editor.

- Under **Render Attributes**, change the **Particle Render Type** to **Cloud**.

5 Change the lifespan mode

- Select the particles.

- Locate the **Lifespan Attributes** section of the Attribute Editor.

- Set **Lifespan Mode** to **lifespanPP only**.

  This forces the particles to obtain their lifespan information from the *lifespanPP* attribute which you will now write an expression for.

6 Add Creation expression to lifespanPP

- With your **RMB** press in the box to the right of the *lifespanPP* attribute in the **Per Particle Attribute** frame.

- Select **Creation Expression...** and add the following expression:

```
lifespanPP = rand(4,6);
```

  This expression sets the lifespan of each particle randomly between 4 and 6 seconds.

Tip:	You don't need to type the particle shape name before the attribute because it is already selected in the **Selection** frame.

- Press **Create** in the Expression Editor.
- **Close** the Expression Editor.

Note:	It is also possible to obtain random lifespans without the use of expressions. Set **Lifespan Mode** to **Random Range** and enter values for **Lifespan** and **Lifespan Random.**

7 Add radiusPP expressions

- With your **RMB** press in the box to the right of the *radiusPP* attribute in the **Per Particle Attribute** frame.
- Select **Creation Expression...** and add the following expression:

```
radiusPP = 0;
```

By default, *radiusPP* has a value of 1. Since you want the particles to start small and grow, you have to explicitly assign the starting (creation) value using this expression.

- In the Expression Editor, click the particle radio button to **Runtime** and enter the following runtime expression:

```
radiusPP = linstep(0, lifespanPP, age);
```

This expression causes the size of the radius to increase linearly from 0 to 1 over the course of the each particle's lifespan.

8 Play the scene

smoothstep **expression**

You will basically do the same thing as you did with the *radiusPP* expression, except this time you will change the opacity so it fades away rather than popping out.

1 Add another attribute to TestPart

- Add an *opacityPP* using MEL.

```
addAttr -ln "opacityPP" -dt doubleArray
    smokePartShape;
```

2 Add an opacityPP expression

- With your **RMB** press in the box to the right of the *opacityPP* attribute in the **Per Particle Attribute** frame.

- Select **Runtime Expression...** and add the following expression:

```
opacityPP = smoothstep((lifespanPP * 0.5),
                              lifespanPP, age);
```

This expression makes the particles start to fade at 0.5, which is at half of their lifespan.

3 Play the scene in shaded mode

What happened? Are your particles fading correctly? The expression is returning a value from 0 to 1, which in this case is transparent to opaque.

Try to edit your `smoothstep` expression by subtracting the result of the `smoothstep` function by 1.

```
smokePartShape.opacityPP = 1 - smoothstep((lifespanPP
                              * 0.5), lifespanPP, age);
```

Now try some variations of your `linstep` and `smoothstep` function expressions:

```
1 - linstep(1, lifespanPP, age);
1 - smoothstep((lifespanPP * 0.2),
                              (lifespanPP * 0.9), age);
```

Tip: You can view the value in any particle attribute by setting the **Particle Render Type** to **Numeric**. Press the **Current Render Type** button and type in the attribute you wish to view in the **attributeName** field. Then press play to see the values displayed.

ANIMATION EXPRESSIONS

Train wheel expression

This is a very simple example of using the motion of one attribute to control another. You will use a simple connection to say, "when the train moves forward, the wheels will turn."

1 Open the file TrainWheelExpression.ma

- Select **File** → **Open Scene**.

- Select the file named *08.TrainWheelExpression.ma*.

2 Create the wheel expression

- Open the Expression Editor.

- Enter the following expression in the Expression Editor:

```
float $fRot = Train.tx * -50;
```

```
frontLeft.rz = $fRot;
secondLeft.rz = $fRot;
thirdLeft.rz = $fRot;
backLeft.rz = $fRot;
```

```
frontRight.rz = $fRot;
secondRight.rz = $fRot;
thirdRight.rz = $fRot;
backRight.rz = $fRot;
```

- Press the **Create** button.

Expression Explanation

The $fRot variable is set equal to Train.tx times -50. This means that as you move the *Train* group in X, a value will be returned and multiplied times -50 to get $fRot.

The remainder of the expression is setting the rotate z value of all the wheels equal to $fRot.

3 Test the results

- **Select** the *Train* group and **Move** it forward along the x axis.

  Notice that the wheels are now moving as you move the Train forward in x.

Swinging sign

You will now open an existing file and review the expression used to swing the lamp sign.

1 Open the file SignLampSwing.ma

- Select **File** → **Open Scene**.
- Select the file named *08.SignLampSwing.ma*.

2 Playback the scene

The sign with the expression should be swinging back and forth around the z axis.

Swinging sign

If you look in the Expression Editor, you will see the expression *SwingingSign*, controlling the motion.

```
float $fAmp = 40;
float $fFreq = 5;
SignExpression.rz = $fAmp * sin(time *$fFreq);
```

Expression Explanation

- The `$fAmp` variable is the amount the sign will swing back and forth.
- The `$fFreq` variable is the speed at which the sign will swing.
- `SignExpression.rotateZ` is the attribute being controlled by the `sin` function you learned about earlier.

3 Apply the same expression to the other sign

- Enter the following expression on the *SignNoExpression* object:

```
float $fAmp = 40;
```

The besselj0 function

Another option for this expression would be the `besselj0` function, which will start off moving then slow to stop over time.

```
float $fFreq = 5;
SignNoExpression.rz = $fAmp * sin(time * $fFreq);
```

4 Test the results

- Playback the scene.

  The signs are now both swinging in the same motion and timing.

Go ahead now and change some of the numbers to see the variations that can be achieved on this simple expression.

Example:

```
float $fAmp = 100 / frame;
float $fFreq = 5;
SignNoExpression.rz = $fAmp * sin(time * $fFreq);
```

or

```
float $fAmp = (1 - smoothstep(0, 10, time)) * 60;
float $fFreq = 3;
SignNoExpression.rz = $fAmp * sin(time * $fFreq);
```

Controlling the sign with Attributes

Another way to control the sign would be to add two attributes to the *SignNoExpression* and have the values in those attributes control the values in the expression.

- Select the object *SignNoExpression* in the Outliner and execute the following in the Script Editor:

  ```
  addAttr -k true -ln "amplitude";
  addAttr -k true -ln "frequency";
  ```

- Edit your expression to the following:

  ```
  float $fAmp = SignNoExpression.amplitude;
  float $fFreq = SignNoExpression.frequency;
  SignNoExpression.rz = $fAmp * sin(time * $fFreq);
  ```

- Now play the scene and try editing the values of *frequency* and *amplitude*.

Swinging lamp

Look at the lamps on the adjoining building in the same scene. When you play the scene, you should see that the motion of the lamps is a little more dynamic. The lamps have a three-dimensional path of motion and swing in x and z.

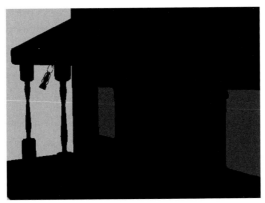

Swinging lamp

If you look in the Expression Editor, you will see the following expression, *SwingingLamp*, controlling the motion:

```
float $fOffset = 1;

float $fFreq = 5;

float $fAmpX = 10;

float $fAmpZ = 30;

LampExpression.rx = $fAmpX * sin(time * $fFreq);

LampExpression.rz = $fAmpZ * sin(time * $fFreq +
                                $fOffset);
```

Expression Explanation

The `$fOffset` is the difference in the motion between X an Z.

The `$fFreq` variable is the speed at which the lamp will swing.

The `$fAmpX` variable is the amount the lamp will swing back and forth in X.

The `$fAmpZ` variable is the amount the lamp will swing back and forth in Z.

The rotate X and Z are both controlled by a `sin` function, with Z having an offset, so that the motion is not perfectly circular.

1 Apply the same expression to the other lamp in the scene

- Enter the following expression on the *LampNoExpression* object:

```
float $fOffset = 1;

float $fFreq = 5;

float $fAmpX = 10;
```

```
float $fAmpZ = 30;

LampNoExpression.rx = $fAmpX * sin(time * $fFreq);

LampNoExpression.rz = $fAmpZ * sin(time* $fFreq +
                                    $fOffset);
```

2 Test the results

- Playback the scene with at least 200 frames in the timeline.

The lamps are now both swinging in the same motion and timing.

Go ahead and change some of the numbers now to see the variations that can be achieved on this expression.

Example:

```
float $fOffset = 1;

float $fFreq = 4;

float $fAmpX = (1 - smoothstep(2, 10, time)) * 50;

float $fAmpZ = (1 - smoothstep(3, 15, time)) * 30;


LampExpression.rx = $fAmpX * cos(time * $fFreq);

LampExpression.rz = $fAmpZ * cos(time * $fFreq +
                                   $fOffset);
```

Blinking railroad light

In this exercise, you will use expressions to control the blinking of a light and the color of a shader.

1 Open the scene file PoleLightBlink.ma

- Select **File** → **Open Scene**.
- Select the file named *08.PoleLightBlink.ma*.

Lights blinking

2 Enter an expression

- Open the Expression Editor.
- Check the following expression:

```
float $fFreq = 2;

float $fIntensity = 2;

PoleLightShape.intensity = sin(time * $fFreq) *
                          $fIntensity;

PoleRedLight.incandescenceR =
                   PoleLightShape.intensity;
```

Expression Explanation

The `$fFreq` variable is the speed at which the light will turn on and off.

The `$fIntensity` variable sets how bright the light will get.

A `sin` curve controls the blinking.

The red incandescence channel is then set to the same value as the intensity of the shader.

3 Switch to hardware lighting

- Press the **7** key to switch to hardware lighting mode.

4 Test the results

- Playback the scene.
- Try to do the same with the green light.

Tip:	You may want to use the `cos` function.

You should also try some variations of the expression to see the results.

Example

```
float $fFreq = 5;

float $fIntensity = 2 * (1 - smoothstep(1, 5, time));

PoleLightShape.intensity = sin(time * $fFreq) *
                              $fIntensity;

PoleRedLight.incandescenceR =
                              PoleLightShape.intensity;
```

Note:	Make sure you have at least 200 frames in the timeline.

Fluorescent light flicker

In this exercise, you will use several `if` statements and the `rand` function to make a light flicker while turning on, similar to the way a fluorescent bulb flickers when turned on.

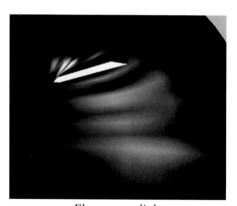

Fluorescent light

1 Open the file TunnelFloorLight.ma
- Select **File** → **Open Scene**.
- Select the file named *08.TunnelFlorLight.ma*.

2 Enter an expression
- Open the Expression Editor.

- Analyze the *LightFlicker* expression.

```
float $fStartTime = 5;

float $fEndTime = 30;

float $fMaxInt = 40;


if (frame > $fStartTime)
{
   if (frame > $fEndTime)
      TunnelLightShape1.intensity = $fMaxInt;
   else
      TunnelLightShape1.intensity = rand(10,$fMaxInt);
}
else
   TunnelLightShape1.intensity = 0;


float $fIntense = TunnelLightShape1.intensity /
                        $fMaxInt;

setAttr LightShader1.incandescence $fIntense
                        $fIntense $fIntense;
```

Expression Explanation

- The $fStartTime and $fEndTime variables are the period in which the light will flicker to turn on.

- The $fMaxInt variable is the intensity of the light when fully turned on.

- The first if statement looks to see if the frame range is past when the light is supposed to turn on. If so, continue to the next if statement.

- The second if statement looks to see if the frame is past when the light should be on. If so turn the light on to the full intensity. If not, do a rand function on the intensity to make the flicker.

- If the first if statement is not past the $fStartTime go to the else statement and make the light intensity equal to zero.

- The setAttr command makes the shader on the light turn to white as the light turns on.

3 Switch to hardware lighting

- Press the **7** key to switch to hardware lighting mode.

4 Test the results

- Playback the scene.
- Try to do the same on the *LighNoExpression* at the other end of the tunnel.

Try some variations of the expression to get different results.

Example:

```
float $fStartTime = 5;

float $fEndTime = 30;

float $maxInt = linstep($fStartTime, $fEndTime,
                            frame) * 40 + 0.0001;


if (frame > $fStartTime)
{
   if (frame > $fEndTime)
      TunnelLightShape1.intensity = $fMaxInt;
   else
      TunnelLightShape1.intensity = rand($fMaxInt);
}
else
   TunnelLightShape1.intensity = 0;


float $fIntensity = TunnelLightShape1.intensity / 40;
setAttr LightShader1.incandescence $fIntensity
                            $fIntensity $fIntensity;
```

MODELING EXPRESSION

Train tracks

You don't often use expressions for modeling, but in this example you will use MEL to place the railroad ties along the train tracks.

1 Open and preview the file

- Select **File → Open Scene**.
- Select the file named *08.TrainTracksExpression.ma*.

2 Playback the scene

- Be sure to set your playback speed to **Play every frame** so that Maya evaluates every frame. Press the **Animation preferences** button at the far right side of the time slider to set this, or select **Window** → **Settings/Preferences** → **Preferences....**

- Set your timeline for **1000** frames.

One railroad tie exists and it will move around the track as the scene plays. This was animated by simply selecting the object then selecting a curve and selecting **Animate** → **Motion Paths** → **Attach to Motion Path**.

3 Enter an expression in the Expression Editor

- Open the Expression Editor.

- Enter the following expression:

```
float $fAmount = 10;
if (frame % $fAmount == 0)
    instance "CrossBar";
```

Expression Explanation

The `$fAmount` variable is the frames between where another bar is placed.

The `if` statement says that if the current `frame` is evenly divided by `$fAmount` then make a instanced copy of `CrossBar`.

4 Test the results

- Playback the scene to see an instanced placed every 10 frames.

Note: As you play the scene, if you let it loop, it will create another set of *CrossBar* over the ones already existing. Make sure to stop the playback before it gets too heavy for your system.

The modulus % symbol

The `%` symbol means the remainder of division. Look at the following example:

```
int $w = 17 / 5;
// Result: 3 //

int $x = 17 % 5;
// Result: 2 //
```

17 can be divided by 5, 3 times. The remainder of 17/5 is 2.

Railroad tracks placed using a modulus expression

Now go ahead and delete all the instances that were created.

Make variations to the expression and play the scene to see the results.

Example:

```
//Pay attention to the int type of $iAmount. If you
//leave it float, the if statement will never be
//true.
int $iAmount = rand(3, 10);

if (frame % $iAmount == 0)
{
    string $instance[] = `instance "CrossBar"`;
    float $fRot = rand(-15, 15);
    rotate -r 0 $fRot 0 $instance[0];
}
```

Tip:	In the last several examples, you covered a variety of ways to use and write expressions. There are a number of other expressions in the Expressions Appendix that you may find useful or at least that will give you ideas on other ways to write expressions.

Example: Manta Ray

It can be very useful to animate one *control object*, then use expressions to feed a slightly altered version of that animation to other objects in the scene. For example, you could animate one leg of a centipede then use that same animation on all the other legs, but have each one slightly offset in time using an expression. This prevents you from having to individually keyframe each leg but keeps the motion relatively the same. Furthermore, you can edit the animation curves for the original control leg and it will update for all the others that are referencing the motion. The following example shows you how to accomplish this kind of task using expressions on joint rotations:

1 Open the example scene

- Open *08.MantaRayStart.ma.*

2 Select the control joint (control_JointR)

- The *control* joint for this skeleton is the third joint back from the front, on the right side of the manta's body.

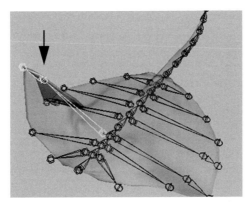

Manta ray with control_JointR selected

- Open the Graph Editor to see the keyframed animation on this joint.

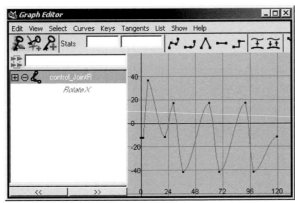

Animation curve for rotateX of control_JointR

3 Add an expression to the opposite joint to mirror motion

The joint directly across from *control_JointR*, *control_JointL*, should have the same exact motion as the control joint except its rotation will be negative instead of positive.

- Enter the following in the Expression Editor and press **Create**:

```
control_JointL.rx = control_JointR.rx * -1;
```

4 Add a time delayed expression

The joint directly behind *control_JointR* is called *oneBackR*. This joint should rotate slightly less than *control_JointR* and slightly later in time.

- Add the following expression below the existing expression you wrote above to accomplish this:

```
$rxMinus3 = (`getAttr -t (frame - 3)
                          control_JointR.rx`);
oneBackR.rx = $rxMinus3 / 1.5;
```

5 Add similar time delayed expressions to remaining joints

Write expressions for the remaining joints in the manta ray using the same method in step 4. Joints further from the front should rotate less and have more of a time delay with respect to the control joint.

Following is the complete expression for controlling all joint rotations in the manta ray. If you get lost, you can refer to them for guidance. Notice that the joint tips are set up to be time delayed from the main joints. The file *08.mantaRayDone.ma* is a completed version.

```
// variable declarations
float $rxMinus2;
float $rxMinus3;
float $rxMinus5;
float $rxMinus7;
float $rxMinus9;
float $rxMinus11;


//Get rotation of main joint and mirror that motion
//to the other side.
control_JointL.rx = control_JointR.rx * -1;


//right control_joint tip on opposite (left) side.
```

```
$rxMinus2 = (`getAttr -t (frame - 2)
                        control_JointR.rx`);
control_JointR_tip.rx = $rxMinus2 * 1.25;
control_JointL_tip.rx = $rxMinus2 * -1.25;


//oneBack from the control joint.
$rxMinus3 = (`getAttr -t (frame - 3)
                        control_JointR.rx`);
oneBackR.rx = $rxMinus3 / 1.5;
oneBackL.rx = ($rxMinus3 * -1) / 1.5;


//oneBackTip
$rxMinus5 = (`getAttr -t (frame - 5)
                        control_JointR.rx`);
oneBackR_tip.rx = $rxMinus5;
oneBackL_tip.rx = $rxMinus5 * -1;


//twoBack
$rxMinus7 = (`getAttr -t (frame - 7)
                        control_JointR.rx`);
twoBackR.rx = $rxMinus7 / 2;
twoBackL.rx = ($rxMinus7 * -1) / 2;


//threeBack
$rxMinus9 = (`getAttr -t (frame - 9)
                        control_JointR.rx`);
threeBackR.rx = $rxMinus9 / 2.5;
threeBackL.rx = ($rxMinus9 * -1) /2.5;


//fourBack
$rxMinus11 = (`getAttr -t (frame - 11)
                        control_JointR.rx`);
fourBackR.rx = $rxMinus11 / 3;
fourBackL.rx = ($rxMinus11 * -1) / 3;


//oneAheadR
```

```
oneAheadR.rx = $rxMinus2 / 1.5;
oneAheadL.rx = ($rxMinus2 * -1) / 1.5;


//twoAheadR
twoAheadR.rx = $rxMinus3 * 1.5;
twoAheadL.rx = $rxMinus3 * -1.5;
```

Exercises

1 A simple expression with `sin`

- Open the file *08.TrainScene.ma.*

- Write an expression with the `sin` function on the arm of the person so that it waves as the scene plays.

2 Add some control to the expression

- Continue with the scene from the first exercise.

- Add attributes to the person that control the:

    frequency (speed of the wave)

    amplitude (size of the wave)

    The attributes should be referenced by the expression to make it as interactive as possible.

3 Reference another object with an expression

- Continue with the scene from the second exercise.

- Write an expression on the coal car so that it follows behind the train.

4 Write a conditional expression

- Continue with the scene from the third exercise.

- Make the `if-else` statement that you wrote in Chapter 6, Exercise 2 into an expression to control the opening and closing of the gate.

5 Create a window that controls the sine frequency

- Continue with the scene from the fourth exercise.

- Create a window with a float slider group and use that slider to control the frequency of the arm wave from the second exercise.

- Modify the expression so it queries the slider for its value.

- Alternatively, reuse that window script and make it control the frequency and amplitude of the signs you worked on in *08.SignLampSwing.ma*.

Summary

You should now be familiar with expressions, how they work, and how they differ from MEL scripts. You should be able to create your own expressions using the Expression Editor and be comfortable with some of the math functions that are available through MEL.

9 Procedures

A procedure is a grouping of MEL commands loaded in memory that can be executed by typing just a single command. As you get into more complex MEL examples, you will find this to be a very helpful tool. With procedures, you can store command statements in memory and call them from script or the command line. You can also pass arguments and get return values from one procedure to another.

In this lesson you will be covering:

- Procedures
- Passing arguments between procedures
- Returning values from a procedure
- Global vs. Local variables

PROCEDURES

You can create a procedure in any way that you want. You can use a simple text editor such as *jot* or *notepad*. You can also write procedures directly in the Script Editor, although, if your procedure is long, you might be better off using your favorite editor and maybe saving it to a file on your disk. Here is the normal form for a simple MEL procedure:

Syntax:

```
proc procedureName()
{
   MELstatements;
}
```

Example:

```
proc hello()
{

   //Print a greeting
   print "Hello world!\n";

}
```

Execution:

```
hello; //Execute the procedure
```

Look at the parts that make up the procedure. First, `proc` stands for *procedure*. You'll begin most procedures with the word `proc`. The *procedureName* is any name you want as long as it does not contain any spaces or special characters and starts with a letter. This is also the name of the command you will type to execute whatever MEL statements are contained in your procedure. As with variables, you need to be descriptive with your choices of names. The `MELstatements` are the commands that you would like to have your procedure execute.

The `fn` "file name" procedure

This procedure simply prints the current file name that you are working on. This is useful when you have the main Maya window up without its title bar.

```
proc fn()
{
   string $fileName = `file -q -sn`;
   print $fileName;
}
```

As you can see, the procedure has a name, *fn*, and it contains two MEL commands.

Declaring procedures

Regardless of how you have created your procedure, for Maya to know about it, you must explain what it does. This is what is referred to as declaring the procedure. Declaring a procedure loads it into Maya's memory so you can then execute it whenever you want during the current Maya session.

1 Declare the `fn` procedure

- Enter the above `fn` procedure into the lower part of the Script Editor.

The procedure in the Script Editor

2 Declare the `fn` procedure so that it can be used

- Press **Enter** on the numeric keypad to execute the whole script.

  The `fn` procedure is now ready to use.

Note: The commands were not executed when you declared the procedure. They were simply stored in Maya's memory for use when you type the name of the procedure into the Script Editor.

Using procedures

Using a defined MEL procedure is the same as using any other MEL command or function. You can execute a MEL procedure in an expression, the command line, or a MEL script; however, the procedure must be declared before it can be used. Since you've already declared the `fn` procedure, now execute it.

1 Execute the `fn` procedure

- Type `fn` into the Script Editor.

▪ Press the numeric **Enter** key to view the current file name.

As soon as you execute the new command `fn`, Maya looks through its memory for some procedure that matches that name. When it finds it, the commands contained within that procedure are executed.

Note: If you get the following error:

    // Error: Cannot find procedure "fn". //

Maya doesn't know yet about the procedure you are trying to execute. It is because you did not declare the procedure correctly. Review the **Declaring Procedures** section.

You can also call a procedure from within another procedure. The following example explains this concept:

```
proc getFileInfo()
{
   fn;
   get_the_in_and_out_frames;
   get_the_number_of_polies;
}

getFileInfo; //Execute the procedure
```

You would get an error executing the above script, since Maya doesn't know about the `get_the_in_and_out_frames` or `get_the_number_of_polies` procedures. MEL doesn't know what to do because the procedures don't exist yet; they have not been declared. In order to correct the problem, you would need to write the new procedures and declare them before the procedure in which they are used, in this case, before the `getFileInfo()` command.

Note: Pay attention to the order of the declaration of procedures. You need to make sure that you don't execute a procedure before its declaration or you would get the following error:

    // Error: Cannot find procedure "someProc". //

To follow the convention, you should declare a procedure before using it in another declaration.

The `hi` and `lo` geometric resolution procedures

These are some simple, yet useful, procedures you can experiment with. These procedures change the display smoothness of all your geometry in the current scene, regardless of what is selected. The `hi` procedure, when executed, changes the display surface to hull (drawn using NURBS rather than control vertices), which offers higher display quality but at the price of lower performance.

```
proc hi()
{
    displaySmoothness -full -du 0 -dv 0 `ls -g`;
}
proc lo()
{
    displaySmoothness -hull -su 2 -sv 2 `ls -g`;
}
```

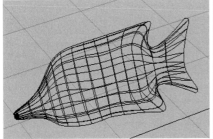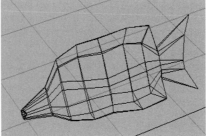

The high and low resolution display

These procedures are to be used in conjunction with the predefined hotkeys **1** through **3**, which change the quality of the display, **1** being the lowest and **3** being the highest. The hi and lo procedures can be executed as follows:

```
hi;
lo;
```

However, it would not make sense to execute them one right after the other.

Automating UI creation with an advanced procedure

Take a look at a few of the things you've learned up to this point. Try and write a slightly more advanced procedure on your own.

You have learned about UI, variables, loops, and procedures. How can you combine all of these things together in one script? And why would you want to?

Suppose that you would really like to create a UI for controlling the translation or rotation of the objects in your scene. It would be a tedious job to do this manually. You would have a large number of scripts just for doing the same thing over and over again.

Using this scenario, you will create a procedure which will create some custom UI for all the selected objects.

1 Declare the procedure in the Script Editor

```
proc controls()
{
    string $sel[] = `ls -sl`;
    string $current;
    for ($current in $sel)
    {
        string $win = `window -t "Controls"`;
        columnLayout;
            attrFieldSliderGrp -min -10 -max 10 -at
                                    ($current + ".ty");
        showWindow $win;
    }
}
```

2 Execute this new procedure

- **Select** two objects.

- Execute the new procedure by typing `controls`.

A new window with a custom control is created for each objects.

By executing the `controls` command, Maya looks into its memory and find the procedure declared in step 1. Next is a review of the commands which are executed by this procedure.

```
string $sel[] = `ls -sl`;
string $current;
```

First, two variables were declared. A string array called `$sel`, to store all the selected objects and a second string variable, called `$current`, which you will use in a `for-in` loop to step through all the items in `$sel`.

```
for ($current in $sel)
{
    string $win = `window -t "Controls"`;
    columnLayout;
        attrFieldSliderGrp -min -10 -max 10 -at
                                ($current + ".ty");
    showWindow $win;
}
```

Using a `for-in` loop, you created a window for every item which was selected. Each window contains one slider which is connected to the translate Y attribute of the selected object.

You can see how, in this example, it is much easier to simply create a procedure than to have to type these commands every single time.

Here's a slightly more advanced example. You'll improve the way you name the window so that it's named the same thing as the object, and you'll add a few more controls:

```
proc controls()
{
   string $sel[] = `ls -sl`;
   string $current;
   for ($current in $sel)
   {
      string $win = `window -t $current`;
      columnLayout;
         attrFieldSliderGrp -min -10 -max 10 -at
                           ($current + ".tx");
         attrFieldSliderGrp -min -10 -max 10 -at
                           ($current + ".ty");
         attrFieldSliderGrp -min -10 -max 10 -at
                           ($current + ".tz");
         attrFieldSliderGrp -min -10 -max 10 -at
                           ($current + ".rx");
         attrFieldSliderGrp -min -10 -max 10 -at
                           ($current + ".ry");
         attrFieldSliderGrp -min -10 -max 10 -at
                           ($current + ".rz");
      showWindow $win;
   }
}
```

Can you think of a way to have all the attributes listed in one window rather than separate windows? On your own, try and improve what was done in the above example. If you get confused, you can check what is done here:

```
proc controls()
{
```

```
string $sel[] = `ls -sl`;
string $current;
string $win = `window -w 450 -h 400 -t Controls`;
scrollLayout;
columnLayout;
   for ($current in $sel)
   {
      text -l $current;
      attrFieldSliderGrp -min -10 -max 10 -at
                         ($current + ".tx");
      attrFieldSliderGrp -min -10 -max 10 -at
                         ($current + ".ty");
      attrFieldSliderGrp -min -10 -max 10 -at
                         ($current + ".tz");
      attrFieldSliderGrp -min -10 -max 10 -at
                         ($current + ".rx");
      attrFieldSliderGrp -min -10 -max 10 -at
                         ($current + ".ry");
      attrFieldSliderGrp -min -10 -max 10 -at
                         ($current + ".rz");
      text -l "";
      text -l "";
      separator -w 450;
      text -l "";
      text -l "";
   }
   showWindow $win;
}
```

ARGUMENTS IN PROCEDURES

Besides creating procedures that just execute MEL statements with no further input from the user, you can require additional user input by using arguments in a procedure. Arguments are values that are supplied to the procedure when it is executed. They are, essentially, just variables. Each argument consists of an argument type and name. You can use multiple arguments in a procedure.

Syntax:

```
proc procedureName(int $i, float $f, string $s)
{
    MELstatements using $i, $f, $s;
}
```

Example:

In the following example, the MEL procedure, `helloValue`, requires an integer and a string argument:

```
proc helloValue(int $value, string $person)
{
    string $greeting = "Hello " + $person +
            ", you are number " + $value + "!\n";
    print($greeting);
}
```

To execute a procedure that has arguments, you must include the values that you want to assign to the arguments. The `helloValue` procedure requires an integer and a string argument, so you would use it like this:

```
helloValue(1, "Jake");
```

will return:

```
Hello Jake, you are number 1!
```

If you simply enter:

```
helloValue;
```

You will get the following error:

```
// Error: Line 1.11: Wrong number of arguments on
call to helloValue. //
```

Note: You don't need the brackets and the comma to specify the arguments of a procedure. The following would work just fine:
```
helloValue 1 Jake;
```
but it is easier to read the arguments if you do add the (,) around them.

RenameAll procedure

You will now update the *renaming* example from Chapter 7 to accept a string argument. Here is the macro you did in that chapter:

```
string $sel[] = `ls -sl`;

string $current;
```

```
for ($current in $sel)
{
    rename $current "ball#";
}
```

First, you must declare a new procedure to execute these commands. You will call the new procedure renameAll. Also, you must pass the procedure a string. This way, you can control what the objects will be renamed without having to edit the commands you are executing.

1 Type the procedure in the Script Editor

```
proc renameAll (string $name)
{
    string $sel[] = `ls -sl`;
    string $current;
    for ($current in $sel)
    {
        rename $current ($name + "#");
    }
}
```

  ■ Press **Enter** on the numeric keypad to declare the procedure.

2 Select the objects you want to rename

3 Execute the procedure

  ■ Enter the following:

```
renameAll "ball";
```

  The objects are renamed to ball1, ball2, ball3, etc.

By passing an argument to the procedure, you have more flexibility in creating your own tools. Rather than having to rewrite a script to deal with different situations, you can just pass different values to the procedure. Here are a few more examples for you to try:

The cww "connection window with" procedure

In one simple MEL command you can bring up the Connection Editor with the left and right sides of the editor pre-loaded with the nodes that you specify in the MEL command.

```
proc cww(string $node1, string $node2)
{
   connectWindowWith $node1 $node2;
}
```

The `fr` "frame range" procedure

This procedure allows you to quickly set the start and end frame of the current playback time range. It is very common for animators to change the current playback time range. This procedure gives you a much quicker way to adjust the time range than using the UI.

```
proc fr(float $minFrame, float $maxFrame)
{
   playbackOptions -min $minFrame -max $maxFrame;
}
```

Returning a value from a procedure

You can also create procedures that return values. Often, when working with procedures, you will want to call one procedure to perform an operation and then return the result. To do this, a return type must be specified between the word `proc` and the procedure name in the declaration. The result is returned by the command `return`, and must be of the same data type defined by the return type.

In the following example, the procedure *multiply* is declared with a return type of integer. After the procedure is done processing its data, it returns the result as the defined return type, which is an integer.

Syntax:

```
proc returnType procedureName()
{
   MELstatements;
   return $something_of_returnType;
}
```

Example:

```
proc int multiply (int $value)
{
   print "Made it to the multiplier procedure\n";
   print ("Value received is : " + $value + "\n");
   return ($value * 2);
}
```

```
proc testPass ()
{
    $initValue = 3;
    print ("Initial value : " + $initValue + "\n");
    print "Calling the multiplier procedure\n";
    $newValue = multiply ($initValue);
    print "Back to the testPass procedure\n";
    print ("Value is now : " + $newValue + "\n");
}
```

- Enter `testPass;` in the Script Editor and look at the output:

```
testPass;

Initial value : 3
Calling the multiplier procedure
Made it to the multiplier procedure
Value received is : 3
Back to the testPass procedure
Value is now : 6
```

The local procedure `multiply`, is called by the procedure `testPass`, by the `$newValue = multiply ($initValue);` line. `multiply` has been declared as a procedure so this line sends `$initValue` to `multiply`. The last line in `multiply`, `return ($value * 2);` multiplies it by two and returns it to `testPass`. Finally, `testPass` continues to the end.

Global and Local variables in procedures

In Chapter 7, you were introduced to the concept of variable scope in terms of programming structures. Now you will look at them in procedures. A *Local* variable is a variable that is defined within a block and accessible only withing the block (its scope). A *Global* variable is declared using the word `global` and is accessible from anywhere in Maya. To declare a variable globally, you would just add `global` to the declaration, as follows:

```
global float $boxHeight;
```

The following procedures uses a variable called `$iRoom`. Notice that `$iRoom` is declared in each procedure:

```
proc kitchen ()
{
    int $iRoom;
    print "Welcome to the kitchen.\n";
    print ("Room #" + $iRoom + "\n");
```

```
}
proc house ()
{
    int $iRoom;
    print "Welcome to the house.\n";
    print ("Room #" + $iRoom + "\n");
    $iRoom = $iRoom + 1;
    kitchen;
}
int $iRoom = 12;
print ("Room #" + $iRoom + "\n");
house;
```

Note: Pay attention to the procedure declaration order.

Look at the output in the Script Editor:

```
Room #12
Welcome to the house.
Room #0
Welcome to the kitchen.
Room #0
```

The room number is different in the procedures than it is outside of the
procedure. Even though the variable has been declared in each procedure,
it is just a *Local* variable. Try the example again, but define $iRoom as a
global variable.

```
proc kitchen ()
{
    global int $iRoom;
    print "Welcome to the kitchen.\n";
    print ("Room #" + $iRoom + "\n");
}
proc house ()
{
    global int $iRoom;
    print "Welcome to the house.\n";
    print ("Room #" + $iRoom + "\n");
    $iRoom = $iRoom +1;
```

```
        kitchen;
    }
    global int $iRoom = 12;
    print ("Room #" + $iRoom + "\n");
    house;
```

This returns:

```
    Room #12
    Welcome to the house.
    Room #12
    Welcome to the kitchen.
    Room #13
```

Declaring $iRoom as a global ensures that all procedures can see it.

Note: You need to be careful when using global variables. You must always put global in front of the variable name so Maya understands that you want the global variable. If you don't use the word global then you run the risk of Maya creating a local variable only within the procedure and not using the value stored in the global variable.

Exercises

1 A simple procedure

- Modify the second exercise of Chapter 7 so that it is a procedure and you can launch the control window from the command line.

2 Procedures

- Create a procedure that will build a window with buttons.
- Each button should have a command that calls a local procedure.
- Here are some ideas for what the window could do:

  Each buttons could create render nodes with useful settings; a spotlight with shadows, an ambient light, a glass shader, a metal shader or a rock shader.

  Build a tree with user defined height, diameter, and type of leaves.

- Make a window that will add particle smoke trails to objects and will control the attributes of the particles after creation.
- Develop a window that will create curves in 3D space that represent the movement of an object. The user should be able to

specify the density of the curve and the time frame that the curve is generated for.

Summary

MEL scripting becomes an extremely powerful tool once you start building your own procedures. A procedure enables you to create a grouping of MEL commands that can be executed by typing just a single command. Procedures can also be structured in such a way that they will accept arguments.

In this Lesson you learned the following:

- Procedures

- Passing arguments to a procedure

- Returning values from a procedure

- Global vs. Local variables

CHAPTER 9
Summary

10 Scripts

A MEL script file is a file that contains MEL commands, MEL procedures, or both. Typically, you use a MEL script file to execute a sequence of commands. For example, you might write a script file to create a wall-shaped object, then apply a brick texture to it.

You can write a MEL script file using a text editor, such as *vi* or *notepad*, then save the MEL script file on disk. MEL script files, by convention, have the extension .mel. You can use script files over and over, for different scenes and in different work sessions. When you execute a MEL script, it does not become part of the scene; therefore, you must execute the script each time you want to repeat the action.

Script files vs. procedures

Although MEL script files and procedures are both places to store MEL commands, they are significantly different. A MEL script file is a file that is physically stored on your hard drive. A MEL procedure is just the definition of your own customized MEL command. This definition can be in Maya's memory, in some editor, or even in a MEL script file. So, procedures can be in script files but a script file can not be in a procedure.

CHAPTER 10

CREATING SCRIPT FILES

To create a script file you would simply create a file ending with .mel that has any number of MEL commands or procedure definitions in it. You can create this file in any way you want, using any text editor. You would then put the script file in a script file location that Maya will find.

Script file location

Most often, user script files are located in the **/maya/scripts/** directory. If your script files are not in this directory, Maya may not be able to find the script file and therefore, it will not automatically be visible to Maya. Maya will indicate that the file does not exist.

If you have multiple versions of Maya installed, you can also store scripts in the folder for its respective version. For example, you could have scripts in **/maya/3.0/scripts/** for version 3.0 scripts or **/maya/4.5/scripts/** for version 4.5 scripts.

You could also have scripts in **/maya/scripts/**, for those you know will work well with any version of Maya.

GLOBAL AND LOCAL PROCEDURES

The words Global and Local will come up when you start getting deeper into MEL scripting. A procedure can be *either* Global or Local. A Global procedure is available to the entire program where as a Local procedure is only available in the block of code that it is defined in. If you created a procedure that produced random numbers, you would want it to be available so any procedures would have access to it and be able to get random numbers. This procedure would be a Global procedure. If you had a procedure that put buttons into a certain window, you would make this a Local procedure since you only want the procedure to be available to one other procedure. You also need to be aware that a Global procedure is held in memory. This can cause memory problems if you have a large number of Global procedures taking up extra memory.

Another issue with Global procedures is naming conventions. When you create a Global procedure it is visible to all other MEL commands. If you happen to name your Global procedure myProc the same name as another procedure myProc then you can encounter problems when myProc is called, since it now has a different definition. If you have loaded your Global procedure myWin after the other myWin procedure was loaded, then you have changed the definition of the procedure. When myWin is called it will probably result in an error.

To define a procedure as Global, you put the word `global` in front of the word `proc` when you are creating the procedure.

Syntax:

```
global proc randomNum()

{

}
```

If you don't want a procedure to be Global, then you just drop the word `global`.

Syntax:

```
proc randomNum()

{

}
```

Global and Local procedures in scripts

When you are creating script files, there are some simple rules that need to be followed in order that the script executes properly. The script needs at least one Global procedure in it. Any other Local procedures have to be at the top of the file.

When a script file is executed, Maya looks in your script directory for a script file that matches the name of the script being executed. It then starts reading this file. It starts at the top and reads down the file until it hits the Global procedure that matches the name of the script file. If you have other Local procedures underneath the Global procedure and they are called by the Global procedure, Maya isn't aware of them yet and would return an error. If those same procedures were moved above the `global proc` then Maya would have to read them in order to get down to the Global procedure. Also, if the script file contains more than one Global procedure, you would need to execute the script file before any of the other Global procedures would be available for use. If you try and call one of the Global procedures before the script is executed, Maya will try and search your scripts directory for a script file with the same name as the executed Global procedure and it will fail. If Maya does not find a script file that matches the name of the procedure, it will fail and this error would be returned:

```
// Error: Cannot find procedure "testProc". //
```

Using a System Call

This example looks for an argument and then does a system call to open a text editor. A system call is a MEL command that gives you control over operating system commands (i.e. IRIX or DOS shell commands) from within a MEL script. This is a very simple script, but it is a great example of how a script does not have to be huge to be useful.

For IRIX

1 Change your current working directory

- In a unix shell window, enter the following:

```
cd ~/maya/scripts/
```

2 Create a text file

- In a unix shell, enter the following:

```
jot edit.mel
```

3 Create the edit script file

- Add the following contents to the edit.mel file:

```
global proc edit (string $name)
{
    system("jot ~/maya/scripts/" + $name +
                        ">/usr/tmp/null 2>&1 &");
}
```

4 Try out your edit script

- After saving the file, type the word edit followed by the name of the script file to edit into the Script Editor, then press **Enter** on the numeric keypad to execute the script.

For Windows

1 Open Notepad

- In the Windows user interface select **Start** → **Programs** → **Accessories** → **Notepad.**

2 Create the edit script file

- Add the following contents to the *Notepad* file:

```
global proc edit (string $fileName)
{
    string $scriptDr = `internalVar -usrScriptDir`;
    system ("start notepad " + $scriptDr + $fileName +
                        ".mel");
}
```

3 Save the file

- Select the **File** menu in *Notepad* and select **Save As.**

- Enter the name `edit.mel` and press **Save.**

4 Try your edit script

- After saving the file, type the word `edit` followed by the name of the script file to edit into the Script Editor, then press **Enter** on the numeric keypad to execute the script.

Creating a shell (IRIX)

1 Change your current working directory

- In a unix shell window, enter the following:

cd ~/maya/scripts/

2 Create a text file

- Enter the following:

```
jot shell.mel
```

3 Create the shell script file

- Add the following contents to the `shell.mel` file:

```
global proc shell()
{
    system("winterm" + ">/usr/tmp/null 2>&1 &");
}
```

4 Try out your shell script

- Save the file and execute the shell procedure in the Script Editor.

Creating a Command Prompt (Windows)

1 Open Notepad

- In the Windows user interface Select **Start** → **Programs** → **Accessories** → **Notepad.**

- Type the following in the content of the file:

```
global proc comPrompt()
{
    system("shell start");
}
```

2 Save the file

- Select the **File** menu in Notepad and select **Save As.**

- Enter the name `comPrompt.mel` and press **Save**.

3 Try your Command Prompt script

- Execute the shell procedure in the Script Editor

An automatic UI creation script file

The following example creates a MEL script file that has an `autoUI` procedure in it. This procedure includes some of the automatic UI creation script that you developed in the previous chapters.

1 Change your current working directory

- In a unix shell window, enter the following:

```
cd ~/maya/scripts/
```

- On Windows, locate the scripts directory in your maya folder.

Note: You could also use your `edit` script from the previous example.

---

2 Create a text file

- In a unix shell, enter the following:

```
jot autoUI.mel
```

- On Windows, you can use *NotePad* to create the `autoUI.mel` file.

3 Create the automatic UI creation script file

- Add the following contents to the `autoUI.mel` file.

```
global proc autoUI()
{
   window;

   scrollLayout;

      columnLayout;
      string $selectedObjects[] = `ls -sl`;

      for ($obj in $selectedObjects)
      {
         text -l $obj;
         checkBox -l "" -onc ("showHidden " + $obj)
                        -ofc ("hide " + $obj);
         attrFieldSliderGrp -min -10 -max 10
                        -at ($obj + ".tx");
         attrFieldSliderGrp -min -10 -max 10
                        -at ($obj + ".ty");
```

```
                    attrFieldSliderGrp -min -10 -max 10
                                       -at ($obj + ".tz");
               }
            showWindow;
        }
```

- Save the file.

You have just made an automatic UI creation MEL script. Now all you need to know is how to use it.

Using script files

There are two ways to use a script file in Maya. You can either execute the script file or you can source the script file. Executing a MEL script file will automatically execute the procedure in that script file that has the same name as the script file. Nothing else besides that procedure will be executed; any other procedures or MEL commands in the script file will not be executed. Sourcing a MEL script file executes all of the MEL commands and declares all the Global procedures that are contained within the script file.

Executing a script file

To execute a script file, there must be at least a Global procedure with the same name as the script file. The preceding examples demonstrates this. One of the files that you created was called `autoUI.mel` and the Global procedure in that same file was called `autoUI`. This makes the script file executable.

- If the automatic UI creation script file is located in the Maya scripts directory, you could execute it by entering the following line in the lower portion of the Script Editor:

  ```
  autoUI;
  ```

- Then press **Enter** on the numeric keypad.

Note: Remember that this example script requires objects to be selected.

Creating a multi Key UI script

The following script contains two procedures. One creates a window, the second is the procedure created after a button is pressed. Place the following into the script called `keyWin.mel` and then execute the script:

```
proc keyFrames()
{
```

```
string $list[] = `ls -sl`;
string $current;
string $keys =`textFieldGrp -q -text values`;
string $buffer[];
string $temp;
$numTokens = tokenize($keys, $buffer);
for($current in $list)
{
   for($temp in $buffer)
      setKeyframe -hi none -cp 0 -s 1 -t $temp
                               $current;
}
}


global proc keyWin()
{
   window;
   gridLayout -nc 2 -cw 400;
      textFieldGrp -l "Keyframes" values;
      button -l "Set Keys on Selected" -w 150
                          -c "keyFrames";
   showWindow;
}
```

To use this UI script, simply select objects and type in the text field what keyframes you want set, separated by spaces.

Sourcing a script file

Sourcing a MEL script file executes all of the MEL commands and declares all Global procedures that are contained within it. To source a script file, use the source command in the Script Editor or the command line. For example, to source the file myScript.mel, enter:

```
source myScript;
```

You do not need to enter the extension .mel if the script is located in your Maya scripts directory. If MEL does not find the file without the extension, it automatically looks for the filename with the .mel extension.

The `source` command can also be used with absolute path names. To do this, however, the argument, which indicates which file is to be sourced, must be contained in a string. The following example illustrates this:

```
source "drive:/somewhere/tempScript.mel";
```

When a MEL script file is successfully sourced, all the MEL commands contained in that file are executed and all the Global procedures in the script are declared, but not executed. Provided there are no errors, the MEL commands are executed in the order in which they appear in the file. If an error is encountered, the file execution halts and no further procedures are loaded.

- For example, sourcing a script file containing this:

```
global proc someProc()
{
    statements;
}
```

  will cause the procedure `someProc` to be *declared*.

- But sourcing a script file containing this:

```
global proc someProc()
{
    statements;
}
someProc;
```

  will cause the procedure to be *declared* and then *executed*.

When sourcing a script file, the procedures are redefined. This means that if you are editing a procedure in a script file, you *must* use the `source` command on that file to update the changes before trying to re-execute it. Maya will then redefine the version of the procedure stored in its memory.

Tip: You can drag a `.mel` file over the Maya workspace to source it easily.

Sharing script files

The ability to share script files is extremely powerful since script files are as portable as any other Maya file. Script files become a means to share utilities, macros, and customized scripts. Since they are just text files, you can send them with email or copy them from one computer to another.

Using script files from others

When you receive a script file that you would like to use, just put the file in your Maya scripts directory. From there, you can either source or execute the file, depending on how it was meant to be used.

Sending script files to others

Sending script files is just as easy as receiving script files. Just send the file or copy it directly to the recipient's Maya scripts directory and they are ready to use the script.

Exercise

- Take the procedures you did in the previous chapter and try to make them into scripts.

Summary

You should now be comfortable with creating, sourcing, and executing script files.

11 Applied Scripts

In the previous two lessons you learned about procedures and scripts, including how to create them. This lesson will take a closer look at the practical use of scripts and procedures and how they can be combined. You will see how you can combine scripts and procedures to create useful utilities to assist in your day-to-day work in Maya. You will also breakdown several scripts to better understand how they work.

In this lesson you will learn the following:

- How to use procedures in scripts in:

    Modeling

    Animating

    Creating UI

    Dynamic effects

- How to create and use effect scripts

- Other Utility Script examples

CHAPTER 11

PROCEDURES IN SCRIPTS

MEL commands in script files are basically macros. When the script file is sourced, all the MEL commands in the script file are executed one after the other. Although it may be useful to use script files as macros, it is much more common to use script files in conjunction with procedures. This gives you capabilities that are just not available with script files that only contain MEL commands.

For example, if you have a procedure with the same base name as a script file, as you learned in the last lesson, you can execute this procedure without sourcing the script file first. This makes executing MEL in script files much simpler than having to use the source command.

You can have several procedures in a single script file. Any of these procedures can be executed by any of the other procedures in the script file provided that they are defined first before they are called. One procedure in the script file can execute any other procedure defined in that script file as many times as you want. This provides modularity and reuse of MEL scripts which, in combination, is very powerful.

To use a script file in conjunction with a procedure, place the procedure in the script file.

Using scripts

To use most scripts, you simply ensure that the script is in your **/maya/scripts/** directory, then just execute it in the Script Editor or on the command line. However, some scripts require a certain number and type of objects to be selected before the script is executed, while others may require arguments to the script procedure.

A script may have several different methods to refine and customize it once it has been executed. These range from modifying added attributes to using an interactive UI.

Creating an emitAway script

In this example, you will create a script file called `emitAway.mel` that has a procedure in it called `emitAway`. This effect creates an emitter at the origin that always emits *away* from the origin. This is a simple effect script that has no options. It shows the basics of creating an effect script and illustrates how easy it is to create one.

1 Create a file in your scripts directory

- Browse to your **/maya/scripts/** directory.

- Create a file called `emitAway.mel` with the following contents:

```
global proc emitAway()
{
    emitter -pos 2 5 3 -type direction -sp 0.3
                            -name emit -r 50 -spd 1;
    particle -name spray;
    connectDynamic -em emit spray
    connectAttr emit.tx emit.dx;
    connectAttr emit.ty emit.dy;
    connectAttr emit.tz emit.dz;
    rename emit "emitAway#";
    rename spray "sprayAway#";
}
```

2 Execute this script

- Save the script and type `emitAway` then **Enter** key on the numeric keypad in the Script Editor or in the command line.

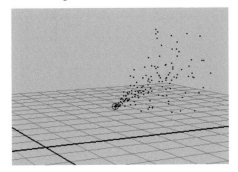

EmitAway particles

Did you get an error?

You would have if you forgot the semicolon at the end of the connectDynamic statement.

- If you got the error, fix the problem, then remember that you will have to `source` the changes you made for Maya to see the new script.

```
source emitAway;
```

- **Move** or keyframe around the `emitAway1` emitter and play the scene to see how it reacts.

Create a chain effect

Now you are going to see how easy it can be to create a simple chain effect, with one argument for the number of links.

1 Start a new scene

- Start a new scene.

- **Clear History** in the Script Editor.

2 Create geometry to represent a chain

- Create a Poly Cylinder on the X axis.

- Create a row of spheres spaced out slightly apart and extending from the end of the cylinder.

3 Add dynamics

- Make all the spheres active rigid bodies.

- Make the cylinder a passive rigid body.

- Connect all of the elements with dynamic hinge constraints.

- Add gravity to the spheres and play the scene.

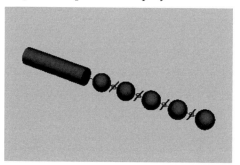

The finished chain

Note: Be sure that **Playback** is set to **Realtime** in the **General Preferences**.

---

4 Reuse the commands to make a script

- Once you are done, cut and paste the commands from the history half of the Script Editor into the lower half.

- Now add the necessary lines to make it into a script. Start another new scene and execute the script that you have created.

```
global proc chain()
{
    polyCylinder -ax 1 0 0;
    scale -r 3 1 1;
    sphere;
```

```
move -r -ls -wd 5 0 0;

duplicate;

move -r -ls -wd 3 0 0;

duplicate;

move -r -ls -wd 3 0 0;

duplicate;

move -r -ls -wd 3 0 0;

duplicate;

move -r -ls -wd 3 0 0;


select -r nurbsSphere1 nurbsSphere2 nurbsSphere3
                       nurbsSphere4 nurbsSphere5;

rigidBody -active -sio sphere;

select -r pCylinder1;

rigidBody -passive;


select -r pCylinder1 nurbsSphere1;

constrain -hinge -o 0 0 0 -i 0;

select -r nurbsSphere1 nurbsSphere2;

constrain -hinge -o 0 0 0 -i 0;

select -r nurbsSphere2 nurbsSphere3;

constrain -hinge -o 0 0 0 -i 0;

select -r nurbsSphere3 nurbsSphere4;

constrain -hinge -o 0 0 0 -i 0;

select -r nurbsSphere4 nurbsSphere5;

constrain -hinge -o 0 0 0 -i 0;


select -r nurbsSphere1 nurbsSphere2 nurbsSphere3
                       nurbsSphere4 nurbsSphere5;

gravity -pos 0 0 0 -m 9.8 -dx 0 -dy -1 -dz 0;

connectDynamic -f gravityField1 nurbsSphere1
                       nurbsSphere2 nurbsSphere3
                       nurbsSphere4 nurbsSphere5;
    }
```

You could also make this into a more flexible script by adding an argument to the script that allows you to enter the numbers of spheres that will be created. There is a completed `chain.mel` located in the **/maya/5.0/ scripts/** folder.

```
global proc chain (int $num)
{
    //NOT NECESSARY. Disable cycle check warnings.
    cycleCheck -e off;

    //create the cylinder and a starting sphere
    polyCylinder -ax 1 0 0;
    scale -r 4 1 1;
    sphere -p 6 0 0;
    duplicate;
    move -r 3 0 0;

    //Duplicate with smart transform. This moves each
    //sphere apart from the previous duplicate with
    //equal spacing. $num-1 is used since one sphere
    //already exists from the above commands.
    for ($i = 1; $i < ($num-1); $i++)
        duplicate -st;

    //Also add the dynamic hinge constraints
    select -r pCylinder1 nurbsSphere1;
    constrain -hinge -o 0 0 0 -i 0;
    select pCylinder1;
    setAttr "rigidBody1.active" 0;

    for ($i = 1; $i < $num; $i++)
    {
        select ("nurbsSphere" + $i);
        select -tgl ("nurbsSphere" + ($i + 1));
        constrain -hinge -o 0 0 0 -i 0;
    }

    select -r rigidHingeConstraint1;
    move -r 1 0 0 ;
```

```
//Connect the spheres to gravity
gravity -pos 0 0 0 -m 9.8 -dx 0 -dy -1 -dz 0;
select "nurbsSphere*";
string $listSpheres[] = `ls -sl`;
connectDynamic -f gravityField1 $listSpheres;

//Adjust some rigid body attributes
for ($i = 1; $i < ($num + 1); ++$i)
{
    setAttr ("rigidBody" + $i + ".standIn") 2;
    setAttr ("rigidBody" + $i + ".bounciness") 0.1;
    setAttr ("rigidBody" + $i + ".damping") 0.2;
}
}
```

The next series of examples is meant for you to see what others have written with MEL. In all of the following examples, the person who wrote each script was not a programmer and each learned MEL by looking at other scripts to get ideas. Look at several different script examples to see how you can use scripts in modeling and animating as well as with dynamics and the UI.

MODELING SCRIPTS

Here you'll see a few examples of scripts used to streamline modeling tasks:

roundedCube.mel

This script creates a cube with rounded edges that has attributes connected to it to interactively adjust the height of the fillets and the size of the cube.

Try executing the roundedCube script and see what happens. Hint, you don't need to do anything before you execute this script.

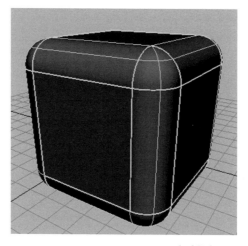
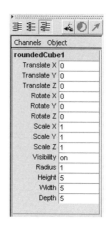

roundedCube

nurbsTorus.mel

This script creates a NURBS Torus shape. Although Maya has a NURBS Torus primitive available, this is a good simple script to learn from. If you open the script, you will see the following in the first Global proc statement:

```
global proc int nurbsTorus( float $minorRadius,
                            int $minorSections,
                            float $majorRadius,
                            int $majorSections )
```

What you can determine by looking at this is that, along with typing in nurbsTorus to execute the script, you need to enter a few other arguments.

float $minorRadius   is looking for a decimal number.

int $minorSections is looking for an integer.

float $majorRadius   is looking for a decimal number.

int $majorSections is looking for an integer.

To run this script you would enter something like the following:

```
nurbsTorus(2.5, 8, 9.8, 12);
```

At the end of this lesson you will find a copy of this script that has been commented so it is very easy to see what the script is doing and how it is accomplished.

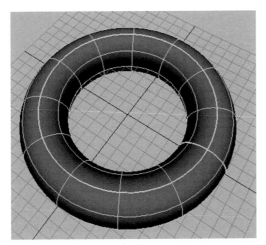

nurbsTorus

ANIMATION SCRIPTS

Following are a variety of script examples that do many things. You can add an expression to a keyframed attribute to create a tool for quickly setting the weights of CV's or lattice points. You can write a script to orient an object to face forward as it moves along.

attrGoalEditor.mel

The first script you will see here is one that was written because the expression that is created by the script was being used frequently for a project. The script opens a UI that allows you to select goal objects and influenced objects and connect them to make the influenced objects follow behind the goal.

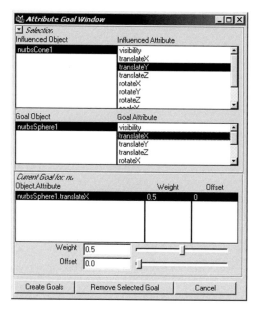

attrGoalEditor

- Create a sphere and a cone.
- Select the sphere and then the cone with the shift key.
- Enter the following into the Script Editor:

  ```
  attrGoalEditor;
  ```
- In the **Influenced Attribute** list select `translateX`.
- In the **Goal Attribute** list select `translateX`.
- You can change the **Weighting** or **Offset** in the lower panel.
- Then simply select **Create Goals**.
- Now set the current frame above 1 and move the goal object back and forth on the X axis.

addMath.mel

This script is very similar to *addExpression* (in your scripts directory and at the end of this lesson), except for the interface that is created. Try to use this script with a simple keyframed ball and figure out what is does.

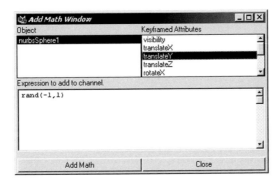

addMath

weightTool.mel

The weightTool utility was created to be a fast version of the Set Editor. In the weightTool dialog box, there is a slider and some quick preset buttons for setting the weight of the selected set components. Whenever the selection changes, the average set weight of the selected components is displayed. There are also buttons for pick-walking CVs and lattice points. This script works on a rigid bound lattice box.

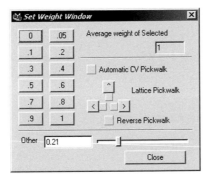

weightTool

forward.mel

The forward.mel script orients the selected object so that it always faces forward as the object moves. It can be used to direct the orientation of objects as they move, such as a school of fish or birds, missiles, blow darts, and so on.

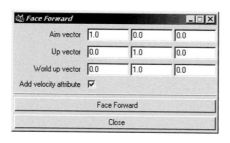
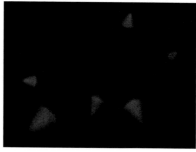

forward

When you execute the `forward` script, a Face Forward dialog box appears. When you click the **Face Forward** button, any selected objects will have expressions added to make them always face whichever direction they are moving.

There is also a check box to add velocity attributes. These attributes give the instantaneous x, y, and z velocity components of the object. You could use these attributes, for example, to change the object's color based on how fast the object is moving.

Working with the forward script

You will use this script to make a cone face forward as you move it.

1 Create a cone

```
cone;
```

2 Execute the forward script

```
forward;
```

3 Add velocity attributes to the cone

- Enable the **Add velocity attribute** checkbox.

4 Apply the face forward script

- Click the **Face Forward** button, then the **Close** button.

5 Test the results

- Move the cone around to see how the `forward` script orients it. Try dragging around the cone, keyframing it, or applying dynamic fields to it.

Tip:	Notice when the cone moves, either by dragging it or otherwise, the velocity attributes update.

USER INTERFACE SCRIPT

Creating a userScripts menu

The `userScripts` script builds a new menu on the main Maya menu bar, called **userScripts**, which contains a menu item entry for each script found in a specified directory on your hard drive.

1 Execute the script

```
userScripts;
```

All the scripts in your **/maya/5.0/scripts/** directory will appear as menu items in the **userScripts** menu.

Note:	The script doesn't search in sub-folders.

2 Select a script from the menu

The corresponding script will be sourced and then executed. This script is designed to work for scripts that do not have an argument list associated with them, so you may encounter errors.

View the contents of `userScripts.mel` to see how to add new menus to Maya's main menubar and also to learn how to have MEL perform different tasks depending which operating system (IRIX or Windows only) the user is running.

DYNAMIC SCRIPTS

Dynamic effects found under the **Effects** menu are really just MEL scripts. However, these MEL scripts were written by experienced programmers and are an excellent source of reference for all kinds of MEL syntax and techniques.

Effects scripts, often written *clipFX*, are pre-made, packaged effects that can be easily applied to enhance a scene. These effects are often created in such a way that any user can quickly get desired effects.

Additionally, these scripts are usually made to be easily modified by the user. You can customize the effect to best suit your specific needs. For example, a fire clip effect may light any selected objects on fire with default settings that control the height, intensity, and scaling of the fire. You may be able to then go in and adjust the settings for these attributes to customize the fire to your liking.

Many effects have their own UI to make them both capable and easy to use. The main point of a clipFX is to save the user a lot of time in making some of the more common effects that can be desired in a scene.

Try out the following effect scripts on the *11.Fullscene.ma* file:

Fire Effect

The fire effect makes selected objects emitters of fire. All of the selected objects will have a common fire, the characteristics of which can altered by adjusting the fire attributes.

This is a great example for writing a robust effect script. What makes this script robust is that it can be applied several times in a scene and to objects that are in an object hierarchy. This effect script is found by default in the Maya installation folder, under **/AliasWavefront/maya5.0/scripts/others/ fireEffect.mel**.

Note: If you want several object fires, each with separate fire control attributes, just select each of the objects and execute fire for each of them.

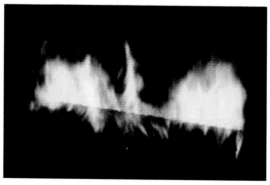

Fire effect

Applying the fire effect

Try applying the fire effect to a sphere. Then, try applying it to several spheres. Finally, try applying different fires to different spheres.

1 **Create a sphere to act as the emitter**

   ```
   sphere;
   ```

2 **Execute the script**

   - With the sphere selected choose **Effects** → **Create Fire.**

3 **Playback the scene**

   You should see fire being emitted from the sphere.

4 **Adjust the attributes**

   - Adjust the attributes added to the particle object. Among these are attributes for controlling the **fire intensity**, **fire lifespan**, **fire turbulence**, **fire density**, and **fire scaling**.

Tip: Select the particles then use the Channel Box to adjust these attributes.

---

5 **Add an ambient light to the scene**

   - Add an ambient light by selecting **Create** → **Lights** → **Ambient Light.**

6 **Software render the fire**

   - Select **Window** → **Rendering Editors** → **Render View...** to bring up the **Render View**.
   - Press the **RMB** in the Render View window and select **Render** → **Render** → **persp** in the pop-up menu.

Bubbles effect

This script makes all the selected objects emit bubbles. To apply this effect, just select the objects that you want to emit bubbles and execute bubble in the Script Editor. The bubbles have extra attributes added to them for controlling the life, emission rate, and scaling of the bubbles.

The bubbles effect script could be used for an underwater scene, a bubble bath, or a carbonated soda.

| Note: | Switch to smooth shaded mode with texturing on by pressing the **6** predefined hotkey. Otherwise, the bubbles appear as just white squares. The bubble texture is in the **sourceimages** directory of the **MF** project. |

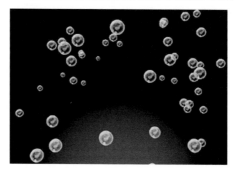

bubbles

OTHER UTILITY SCRIPTS

copyAttr.mel

This script makes it easy to copy attributes from one selected object to another. This is most useful for copying shader attributes between different shading groups, but can be used for camera attributes and other nodes as well. Below is a quick example of the script's usage:

- Create two **shaders** in the Hypershade.
- Type `copyAttr` in the Script Editor.
- Drag and drop one shader into each side of the resulting window.
- Change the **color** of the first shader.

- Select the *color* attribute for both shading groups in the copyAttr window and press the **Copy Attribute** button to copy the changed color to the second shading group.

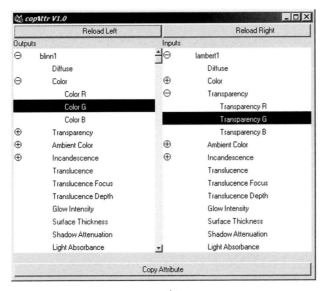

copyAttr

This script uses the `paneLayout` which is the same layout Maya's Connection Editor is based on. MEL commands check what data type is selected on the left and ensures that the data type on the right is compatible. Multiple attributes can be copied simultaneously. This script also has some good example usage of conditional statements and logical operators.

panelOptions.mel

This simple script keeps your modeling window display options the same in all modeling panels when you switch layouts. To see how this works, do the following:

1 Add 2 saved layouts to your shelf

- Press **Ctrl + Shift**, go in **Windows → Saved Layouts** and select **Single Perspective View** to add it to your shelf.

- Repeat the operation for **Four View**.

2 Edit the shelf commands

- Edit the MEL commands in the Shelf Editor for the resulting shelf buttons so they read as follows:

    For the **Single Perspective View** shelf button:

    ```
    panelOptions "Single View";
    ```

    For the **Four View** shelf button:

    ```
    panelOptions "Four View";
    ```

3 Testing the script

- Create a poly sphere, a NURBS sphere and add a light to the scene.
- In the **Show** menu of your perspective window, uncheck **NURBS Surfaces** and **lights**.
- Click in the persp window to give it focus, then click one of the shelf buttons you created. Notice that the shading and show menus in the four views all match, whereas without this script, each checklist in each menu would need to be set manually.

COMMENTED SCRIPTS

nurbsTorus

```
// Description : To create a NURBS torus primitive.
// Modelling Cmd used : nurbs circle and revolve.
// Usage :
//        nurbsTorus(minorRadius, minorSections,
//                    majorRadius, majorSections)
// Example : nurbsTorus(0.5, 4, 0.5, 10)

// The generating circle of radius 'minorRadius' is
// created with centre ($majorRadius + $minorRadius,
// 0, 0), normal (0,0,1) and number of sections
// 'minorSections'. The circle is revolved to
// generate the torus.


global proc int nurbsTorus( float $minorRadius,
                            int $minorSections,
                            float $majorRadius,
                            int $majorSections )
{
    int $ec = 0;
    int $circleCreated = 1;
    int $torusCreated = 0;
```

```
// 1. Create the generating circle with -ch false
// on the XZ plane
string $genCircle[];


float $xc = $minorRadius + $majorRadius;
if( catch( $genCircle = `circle -ch false
                        -nr 0 0 1 -c $xc 0.0 0.0
                        -s $minorSections -d 3
                        -r $minorRadius` ))

   $circleCreated = 0;


// 2. Revolve the circle about the +Z axis,
// -ch false


string $torus[];
if( $circleCreated == 1 )
{
   $torusCreated = 1;
   if( catch( $torus = `revolve -ch 0 -s $majorSections -p 0 0 0
                                -axis 0 1 0 $genCircle[0]` ) )
   {
      $torusCreated = 0;
   }
}
if( $circleCreated == 1 )
   delete $genCircle[0];
if( $torusCreated )
   select -r $torus[0];
return $torusCreated;
}
```

IKdisableWin

```
// Procedure Name: IKdisableWin

// Description:
//    This script creates a window for enabling or disabling IK handles
//    When an IK handle has been selected, you push the button in the
```

```
//    window and it selects all the joints associated with it,
//    then disables or enables the IK handle and sets keyframes on
//    everything selected.

// This procedure selects the joints associated with an IK handle. Sets
// keyframes on the IK handle and the joints. It then disables or
//enables the IK handle.

global proc ikOnOff()
{
   //get a listing of any active IK handles
   string $activeIKHandle[] = `ls -sl -type "ikHandle"`;


   //check to see if an IK handle is selected if it is not prompt
   //the user to select one
   if (size($activeIKHandle) == 0)
   {
      print "Please pick an IK Handle";
   }


   //if the user has picked an IK handle do the following
   else
   {
      //A for loop is needed in case more than one IK handle is selected
      for ($activeIK in $activeIKHandle)
      {
         //We need to make sure that only one IK handle is selected
         select $activeIK;


         //We need to be able to pick the joints that are contained
         //within the IK handle.The listConnections command is used to
         //see what joints are connected to the IK handle.
         string $endEffector[] = `listConnections -type "ikEffector"`;
         string $lastJoint[] = `listConnections -type "joint"
                                                      $endEffector`;
         string $firstJoint[] = `listConnections -type "joint"`;


         //Add the first and last joints to the selection and
         //then put the result in a variable
         select -add $lastJoint $firstJoint;
```

```
string $selectAll[] = `ls -sl`;

select $lastJoint;

$lastJoint = `ls -sl`;


//Pick the last joint and then use pickWalk to go up to the
//first joint using a while loop. Keep adding the new joint to
//the selection
while ($firstJoint[0] != $lastJoint[0])
{
   string $newSelection[] = `pickWalk -d "up"`;

   select $selectAll $newSelection;

   $selectAll = `ls -sl`;

   select $newSelection;

   $lastJoint = $newSelection;

}


// Select IK handle and the joints and set keyframes on them
select $selectAll;

setKeyframe;


//Enable or disable the IK handle. First check to see if the IK
//handle is on or off
if (`getAttr ($activeIK + ".solverEnable")` == 1)
{
   //if the IK handle is on turn it off by changing the
   //attribute
   setAttr ($activeIK + ".solverEnable") 0;

   print ($activeIK + "'s solver has been disabled\n");

}
else
{
   //if the IK handle is off turn it on by changing
   //the attribute
   setAttr ($activeIK + ".solverEnable") 1;

   print ($activeIK + "'s solver has been enabled\n");

}
}
```

```
        //After running all the above return the selection to the original
        //IK handles
        select $activeIKHandle;
    }
}


//Create a window with a button
global proc IKdisableWin()
{
    string $wind = "IKdisable";

    //Check and see if the window exists
    if (!`window -exists $wind`)
    {
        window -width 150 -title "Disable/Enable IK" $wind;
        columnLayout -adjustableColumn true;
            button -label "Disable/Enable" -command "ikOnOff";
        showWindow $wind;
    }
}
```

addExpression script

```
// Procedure Name: addExpression
// Description:
//    This script is used to add an expression to, perhaps, already
//    keyframed object attribute.  This way you can combine keyframing with
//    expressions.
//
//    To use this script just select the objects and attributes that you
//    want to add an expression to in the Channel Box and execute
//    addExpression.
//
//    This script provides procedures to add an expression to an attribute
//    that may be already controlled by a keyframe.  A new attribute is
//    added to the object with the same name as the original attribute
//    but it is prepended with "base".  Any keyframes on the original
//    attribute is moved to this new base attribute.  Finally, a simple
//    expression is created that makes the original attribute equal to
//    the base attribute.
//
// Input Arguments:
```

```
//    Attribute selected in Channel Box.
// Return Value:
//    None.

// This procedure adds an expression to the passed in object attribute.
global proc addExpr(string $object, string $attribute)
{
    // Transform the attribute name to its corresponding long name if it
    // exists.  If it does not exist then give a warning and return.
    string $temp[];
    if (catch($temp = `listAttr ($object + "." + $attribute)`))
    {
        warning("Cannot add expression to " + $object + "." +
                                            $attribute + ", not
found.");
        return;
    }
    else
        $attribute = $temp[0];


    // Since the object name is assumed to be in its long form
    // (eg:  |groupA|nurbsSphere1) we need the short form of the object name
    // (eg:  nurbsSphere1) to use as a base name for the expression that
    // connects the attribute to an added one.  Make the name, the object
    // name, plus the capitalized version of the attribute name, plus "Expr".
    tokenize($object, "|", $temp);
    string $name = $temp[size($temp) - 1];
    string $Attribute = toupper(substring($attribute, 1, 1));
    $Attribute += substring($attribute, 2, size($attribute));
    $name += $Attribute + "Expr";


    // Make the name of the new attribute to be "base" plus the
    // capitalized version of the attribute name.  Also, create the
    // expression string which is just makes the passed in attribute equal to
    // the new attribute.
    string $newAttribute = "base" + $Attribute;
    string $expression = $attribute + " = " + $newAttribute + ";";
    $attribute = $object + "." + $attribute;
```

```
// Make the attribute name fully specified and then add a duplicate
// attribute to the passed in one but under the new name.
string $type = `getAttr -type $attribute`;
int $keyable = `getAttr -keyable $attribute`;


// Get the number of sources and if the passed in attribute is
// keyframed.
int $sources = size(`listConnections -plugs true -source true
                                    -destination false $attribute`);
int $keyframed = `keyframe -query -keyframeCount $attribute` > 0;


// If there are no sources or the attribute is keyframed then we can
// add an expression to the attribute.
if ($sources == 0 || $keyframed)
{
   // Make the new attribute keyable if the passed in
   // attribute was and then make sure that the passed in
   // attribute is not keyable.
   addAttr -longName $newAttribute -attributeType $type
                             -defaultValue (`getAttr $attribute`) $object;
   setAttr -e -keyable $keyable ($object + "." + $newAttribute);
   setAttr -e -keyable false $attribute;


   // If the attribute is keyframed then move the keyframes to the
   // new attribute.
   if ($keyframed)
   {
      cutKey -time ":" $attribute;
      pasteKey -option replaceCompletely -attribute $newAttribute $object;
   }


   // Create the expression on the object.
   expression -name $name -string $expression -object $object;
}
else
   warning("Cannot add expression to " + $attribute +
                            ", controlled by other than keyframing.");
```

```
   // Force a refresh of the channel box by making a phony selection.
   select -tgl time1;
   select -tgl time1;
}


// This procedure calls addExpr for each selected attribute of the
// objects, shapes, and history objects in the Channel Box.
global proc addExpression()
{
   // Set the name of the main Channel Box and get the selected objects and
   // shapes in it.  Also, turn on the wait cursor.
   waitCursor -state on;
   string $channelBox = "mainChannelBox";
   string $objects[] = `channelBox -query -mainObjectList $channelBox`;
   string $shapes[] = `channelBox -query -shapeObjectList $channelBox`;
   string $historyList[] = `channelBox -query -historyObjectList
                                                          $channelBox`;


   // Get the selected attributes and shape attributes in the Channel Box.
   string $attributes[] = `channelBox -query
                                  -selectedMainAttributes $channelBox`;
   string $shapeAttributes[] = `channelBox -query
                                  -selectedShapeAttributes $channelBox`;
   string $historyAttributes[] = `channelBox -query
                                  -selectedHistoryAttributes $channelBox`;


   // If there are no attributes selected in the channel box then give a
   // warning.
   if (size($attributes) + size($shapeAttributes) + size($historyAttributes)
                                                                       < 1)
   {
      warning("Select an attribute in the Channel Box to add an " +
                                                  "expression to.");
   }


   // Add an expression to each selected attribute for each object in the
   // Channel Box.
```

```
string $object, $attribute;
for ($object in $objects)
   for ($attribute in $attributes)
      addExpr($object, $attribute);


// Add an expression to each selected attribute for each shape object in
// the Channel Box.
string $shape;
for ($shape in $shapes)
   for ($attribute in $shapeAttributes)
      addExpr($shape, $attribute);


// Add an expression to each selected attribute for each history object
// in the Channel Box.
string $history;
for ($history in $historyList)
   for ($attribute in $historyAttributes)
      addExpr($history, $attribute);


// Turn off the wait cursor.
waitCursor -state off;
}
```

12 ScriptJob & Script Node

This section discusses the `scriptJob` MEL command and the script node functionality found in the Expression Editor.

You will learn the following in this lesson:

- What is a script job?
- How to view current script job processes
- How to start and kill a script job
- `scriptJob` applications, `smartUI` and `userSetup.mel` tricks
- What is a script node?
- Displaying an information window using a script node

ScriptJob listing

WHAT IS A SCRIPT JOB?

A script job is a MEL invoked process that Maya runs to *listen* for a specific action or *event* to occur. Script jobs are very useful for triggering a script or commands when a specific action takes place.

Perhaps you want to run a script you wrote that displays a window, but you only want this window to be displayed under certain conditions, for example, when a specific object is selected, or when the selection list changes, or when the user changes tools. These, and many others, are *events* that can be monitored and responded to using the scriptJob MEL command.

Script Job basics

When Maya starts, a number of script jobs get started automatically. Think of script jobs as similar to a background process in an operating system, with the added functionality that they can respond to conditions defined by the user. Each script job has a process ID associated with it. To view the script jobs that Maya currently has running, type the following in the Script Editor:

```
scriptJob -listJobs;
```

Notice the output in the history window of the Script Editor showing a unique process job number next to each job.

Script Job Example One: "New Scene" Setup

Perhaps you want the contents of a specific script to be executed every time you create a new scene file. This is a good application for a simple scriptJob command.

1 Start the script job

```
scriptJob -event "NewSceneOpened" "setup";
```

The script job started above executes the setup.mel script every time a new scene is opened. The setup.mel script could be any MEL script and it doesn't need to be named *setup*.

2 Confirm that the scriptJob is running

```
scriptJob -listJobs;
```

3 Create a New scene

- Select **File → New Scene.**
- Look in the Outliner for default lights in your scene to confirm that the setup.mel file was executed.

`Setup.mel` has a variety of different things such as automatic default lighting and predefined render global settings written into it. You can customize the `setup.mel` file (in your scripts directory) to give you the settings you use most often.

userSetup.mel script file

As discussed in an earlier lesson, `userSetup.mel` is a file in your scripts directory that gets executed when Maya is launched.   This is a good way to get script jobs started in your scene right from the start. If you put the `scriptJob` command from above into `userSetup.mel` than that script job will be started every new session of Maya (all script jobs are killed when Maya exits).

Note: `userSetup.mel` does not exist by default. If it is not in your scripts directory, you'll need to create it with a text editor.

What events can a script job listen for?

There is a predefined list of things that the `scriptJob` command can be set to monitor for. For a complete list of these events, type:

```
scriptJob -listEvents;
```

For a description of each event, refer to the on-line MEL command reference for the `scriptJob` command.

Killing a script job

Once a script job is created, you can stop it by typing:

```
scriptJob -kill jobNumber;
```

For example, to kill job number 38:

```
scriptJob -kill 38;
```

Script Job Example 2: smartUI.mel

In a previous lesson, you created an `autoUI.mel` script that would construct a window with sliders to control the selected object. This example takes it one step further by making the window dynamically rebuild based on the contents of the selection list. This prevents you from having to relaunch the script every time your selection list changes.

1 Open legs.ma

2 Source and execute smartUI.mel

```
source smartUI;

smartUI;
```

You may want to drag the above two commands to your shelf so you can easily launch the smartUI window as you work. This script must be sourced before executing properly.

3 Change the selection list

- Select *left_ankleLocator* and watch the smartUI refresh.
- Now select *right_ankleLocator* handle to see the smartUI rebuild.
- You can also select multiple objects and controls for all of them will be built in the window.

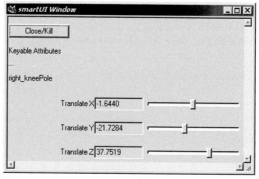

smartUI

4 Kill the script jobs

- Press the **Close/Kill** button in the smartUI window to kill the smartUI script jobs.

Note: If you close the window without the **Close/Kill** button, as soon as you change the current selection, the window will appear because the script jobs were not killed.

How are script Jobs used in smartUI.mel?

Open smartUI.mel from your scripts directory with a text editor. This script is comprised of three procedures: deleteTheUI, killJobs and smartUI. At the beginning of the smartUI procedure, two script jobs are created.

```
//Start the script jobs if they don't already exists
//and store their numbers in global variables so they
//can be killed later.
global int $g_job1, $g_job2;

//make sure there is not already that scriptjob
//before creating it
string $jobs[] = `scriptJob -listJobs`;
int $createJob1 = yes;
int $createJob2 = yes;
for($each in $jobs)
{
   if(`gmatch $each
           "*\"SelectionChanged\"*\"smartUI\"*"`)
     //it exists! Don't create the job 1
     $createJob1 = no;
   if(`gmatch $each
           "*\"SomethingSelected\"*\"deleteTheUI\"*"`)
     //it exists! Don't create the job 2
     $createJob2 = no;
}
if($createJob1 == yes)
   $g_job1 = `scriptJob -event "SelectionChanged"
              "smartUI"`;
if($createJob2 == yes)
   $g_job2 = `scriptJob -conditionFalse
              "SomethingSelected" "deleteTheUI"`;
```

The process ID of each script job gets stored in the Global variables $g_job1 and $g_job2 so these jobs can be killed later. When the selection changes, the smartUI procedure is invoked and the UI is built with whatever is in the selection list.

The second scriptJob uses the -conditionFalse flag to say "if there *isn't* anything selected, call the deleteTheUI procedure". A button is created that calls the killJobs procedure. This kills the two running script jobs so the window doesn't keep popping up.

Another way to approach this, which is a little bit more complex, would be to not use Global variables. By changing the killJobs procedure to accept two integer arguments, you could have passed explicitly the job numbers to the `killJobs` procedure as follow:

```
button -label "Close/Kill" -w 100
    -c ("killJobs (" + $job1 + ", " + $job2 + ")")
    killButton;
```

Tip: It is also common to use the -parent flag in your `scriptJob` statement. This will parent the script job to a specified piece of UI so the script job is killed when the UI is deleted or closed.

SCRIPT NODES

Script nodes provide a method of associating or embedding a MEL script with a scene file.

There are times when you want a script to be associated with a specific file. For example, perhaps you want a series of character UI scripts to be invoked when your character files are opened and a series of lighting UI scripts to be invoked for other files you are working with.

Script Node Example: Information Window

To illustrate the process of using a script node, you will build a UI window with text describing the contents of the file. This window will be displayed whenever the file is opened.

1 Open the Expression Editor

- **Window → Animation Editors → Expression Editor...**

2 Switch to script node edit mode

- Select **By Script Node Name** from the **Select Filter** menu in the Expression Editor

   This sets the Expression Editor for viewing and entering commands associated with script nodes instead of expressions.

3 Enter MEL commands to create a window

- Enter the following commands in the Expression Editor:

```
if (`window -ex "infoWin"`)
     deleteUI infoWin;

window -resizeToFitChildren true
                -topLeftCorner 174 11
                -title "scriptNodeWindow" infoWin;
```

```
columnLayout;
    text -label "This file shows you how ";
    text -label "to set up new attributes and ";
    text -label "connect them with MEL commands ";
    text -label "";
    button -label "Close" -command "deleteUI infoWin";
showWindow infoWin;
```

- Press **Create**.

4 Adjust the script node settings

- Set the script node name to *infoWinScriptNode* and press Enter.

- Set **Execute on:** to **Open/Close.**

  This causes these MEL commands to be executed when it is loaded.

5 Save and reopen the file

- Save the file.

- Reopen the file to see the window displayed in the upper left corner.

The script node has many applications but the process is the same. Script nodes are good for executing per frame commands before each frame is software rendered. For example, you could have a script that checks available disk space on the system and redirects images to another volume if disk space gets low.

Tip: You can also create, edit, and query script nodes using the `scriptNode` MEL command.

Summary

Script jobs provide many new possibilities for what you can do with MEL. Become familiar with the full list of available *events* and always keep them in mind as a possible solution when planning the development of your scripts.

Script nodes give you a simple method of associating a script with specific scene files. Use them anytime you need to save the contents of a script within the file.

In this lesson the following key points were covered:

- What is a script job?
- How to view current script job processes
- How to start and kill a script job
- `scriptJob` applications, `smartUI` and `userSetup.mel` tricks
- What is a script node?
- Displaying an information window using a script node

A UI Appendix

WINDOW MANAGEMENT

Listing UI elements revision

A problem that can arise when creating UI is the existence of naming conflicts. Certain UI elements require a unique name. For example, if you try to create a window named *myWindow* when another window with the same name exists, Maya will return an error stating that your UI object's name is not unique. The solution to the problem is to list all the existing windows with the following command and then use conditional statements to determine if the window exists. If it does already exist then it can either be edited or deleted and rebuilt.

```
lsUI -windows;
```

Some of the other flags for this command are as follows:

-panels	All currently existing panels.
-editors	All currently existing editors.
-controls	Controls created using ELF UI commands. [e.g. buttons, checkboxes, etc]
-menus	Menus created using ELF UI commands
-menuItems	Menu items created using ELF UI commands

Note: ELF UI stands for : Extended Layer Framework User Interface.

Deleting UI elements revision

UI elements are deleted using the `deleteUI` command. Most UI objects are automatically deleted if their parents are deleted. However, some UI objects like the modelPanel will not be automatically deleted and will require the deleteUI command.

Here is an example of how you would use the deleteUI command:

```
window winName;
columnLayout;
    button -label "Button Label" buttonName;
showWindow;
```

Use the following to delete the button:

```
deleteUI buttonName;
```

Executing the following command will delete the window and its content:

```
deleteUI winName;
```

Editing UI elements revision

Existing UI elements can also be edited, without rebuilding the entire UI. As long as you name these elements, they can be changed or queried at any time.

Note: There are ways to retrieve UI element names using `lsUI` or the flag `-childArray` on layouts, but it is a difficult task. You are better off naming everything as you go.

For example, executing the following script creates a simple window with a button:

```
window -title "Test Window" winName;
columnLayout;
    button -label "Button Test" -w 50 buttonName;
showWindow;
```

Use the following to edit that same button:

```
button -edit -w 200 buttonName;
```

When editing a control or a window, you must always include the `-edit` flag and the name of the element.

Parents and children revision

You will see the terms *parent* and *child* used in relation to UI elements and
ELF commands. In this context, a parent is simply a UI element that
contains other UI elements and a child is an element that is contained
within a parent. A child of one parent may also be the parent of other
children just like a hierarchy. Windows are the top-most parent of the
hierarchy. Other elements in the hierarchy can be layouts, controls, menus,
menu items, etc. The hierarchy can be arbitrarily deep as layouts can
contain other layouts and menu items can contain sub-menus.

LAYOUT TYPES

Form layout

One of the more powerful layouts is the `formLayout`. This layout supports
absolute and relative positioning of child controls. For example, you may
specify that a control's position remains fixed while its dimensions are
relative to the size of the window. This concept is best illustrated with the
following example:

```
window -widthHeight 300 200 -t "formLayout example";

formLayout testUI;

    button -label A b1;
    button -label B b2;
    button -label C b3;
    button -label D b4;
    button -label E b5;

formLayout -edit

    -attachForm              b1      "top"     5
    -attachForm              b1      "left"    5
    -attachControl           b1      "bottom"  5 b2
    -attachPosition          b1      "right"   0 75


    -attachNone              b2      "top"
    -attachForm              b2      "left"    5
    -attachForm              b2      "bottom"  5
    -attachForm              b2      "right"   5


    -attachOppositeControl   b3      "top"     0 b1
    -attachPosition          b3      "left"    5 75
    -attachNone              b3      "bottom"
    -attachForm              b3      "right"   5
```

```
-attachControl            b4      "top"      0  b3
-attachOppositeControl    b4      "left"     0  b3
-attachNone               b4      "bottom"
-attachOppositeControl    b4      "right"    0  b3


-attachControl            b5      "top"      0  b4
-attachOppositeControl    b5      "left"     0  b4
-attachNone               b5      "bottom"
-attachOppositeControl    b5      "right"    0  b4
    testUI;
showWindow;
```

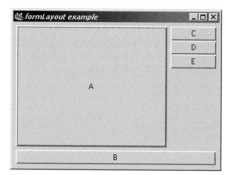

Examples of the same formLayout

Multi-layout window

This example combines several types of layouts, some of which we have covered and others that we have not. If you have any questions about the flags used or the reasons for the parenting, refer to the **MEL user guide** → **Creating Interfaces** section in the help documentation.

```
window -t "Multiple layouts example"
                        -resizeToFitChildren true;
columnLayout -adjustableColumn true;
    frameLayout -label "Buttons" -cll true;
        columnLayout;
            button; button; button;
            setParent ..;
        setParent ..;
    frameLayout -label "Scroll Bars" -cll true;
        columnLayout;
```

```
            intSlider; intSlider; intSlider;
            setParent ..;
        setParent ..;
    gridLayout -numberOfColumns 3
                            -cellWidthHeight 50 50;
        button; button; button; button;
        setParent ..;
    separator -style "double" -w 30 ;
        text "This is a test";
showWindow;
```

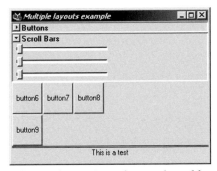

A window with a variety of controls and layouts

USEFUL UI METHODS

Attaching commands to UI elements

The types of actions that are supported for each control depend upon the nature of that control. For example, buttons only support the execution of a command when they are pressed, whereas sliders support commands when they are dragged and also when they change value. See the command documentation for the list of callbacks supported by each control.

A simple example is to attach a command to a button. The following command will change the button's label text when the button is pressed:

```
window -title "Test Window";
    columnLayout;
        button -label "Initial Label" tmp;
```

```
button -edit -command
    ("button -edit -label \"Final Label\" tmp")
    tmp;
showWindow;
```

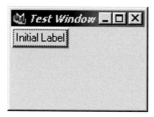 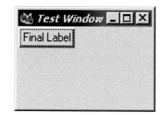

A button that changes its label when pressed

In this example, a single command is attached to the button. It is equally easy to attach procedures with arguments. The following example slightly modifies the above example:

```
window -title "Test Window" win;
columnLayout;
    string $button = `button -label "Initial Label"`;
    button -edit -command
            ("changeButtonLabel " + $button) $button;
showWindow;


proc changeButtonLabel (string $whichButton)
{
    string $labelA = "New Label A";
    string $labelB = "New Label B";
    string $currentLabel = `button -query -label
                            $whichButton`;

    if ($currentLabel != $labelA)
        button -edit -label $labelA $whichButton;
    else
        button -edit -label $labelB $whichButton;
}
```

Adding menus

We can also add UI to the already existing Maya interface or to UI that we have created. Adding menu bars to a UI can clean interfaces with a lot of information in them. For example, you may not like the **File Save** window and decide to get ambitious and write a new one. You would want to have menus for all your new options.

```
window -menuBar true TestWindow2;

    menu -label "File" TestFileMenu;

        menuItem -label "Open"  menuItem1;
        menuItem -label "Close" menuItem2;
        menuItem -label "Quit"  menuItem3;

    menu -label "Edit" TestEditMenu;

        menuItem -label "Cut"   menuItem1;
        menuItem -label "Copy"  menuItem2;
        menuItem -label "Paste" menuItem3;

    menu -label "Options" TestOptionsMenu;

        menuItem -label "Color" -subMenu true
                                          menuItem1;

        menuItem -label "Red";
        menuItem -label "Green";
        menuItem -label "Blue";

        setParent -menu ..;

        menuItem -label "Size" -subMenu true
                                          menuItem2;

        menuItem -label "Small";
        menuItem -label "Medium";
        menuItem -label "Large";

        setParent -menu ..;

    showWindow;
```

A window with menus and sub-menus

Confirm dialog box

A confirm dialog provides a message and user definable buttons through the `confirmDialog` command. When the dialog is dismissed the command returns which button was selected. For example, the following command will produce the dialog shown below:

```
confirmDialog -message "Are you sure?"
              -button "Yes"
              -button "No"
              -defaultButton "Yes"
              -cancelButton "No"
              -dismissString "No";
```

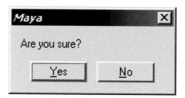

A confirm dialog

This is an example of how to use `confirmDialog`:

```
string $answer = `confirmDialog
                  -message "Are you sure?"
                  -button "Yes"
                  -button "No"
                  -defaultButton "Yes"
                  -cancelButton "No"
                  -dismissString "No"`;
if($answer == "Yes")
    print "User said Yes!\n";
else
    print "User said No.\n";
```

Prompt dialog box

A prompt dialog works similarly to a confirm dialog except that it also provides an editable scrolling field through which the end user can reply to the prompted question. For example, the following command will produce the dialog shown below:

```
promptDialog -message "Enter name:"
             -button "Ok"
             -button "Cancel"
```

```
                -defaultButton "Ok"
                -cancelButton "Cancel"
                -dismissString "Cancel";
```

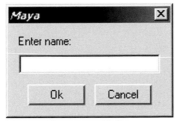

A prompt dialog

After the user enters information into the dialog and presses **OK**, the information entered can be queried and used in a script or an expression.

```
string $answer = `promptDialog -message "Enter name:"
                    -button "Ok"
                    -button "Cancel"
                    -defaultButton "Ok"
                    -cancelButton "Cancel"
                    -dismissString "Cancel"`;

if($answer == "Ok")
{
    print (`promptDialog -q` + " !!!\n");
}
else
    error "Cancelled by user.";
```

EXAMPLES OF MORE COMPLEX UI

Weight tool window

This is a simplified example of a more complex form layout. In the actual working version of this window, command lines would be added to all the buttons and all the checkboxes would be queried to find their state. The working `weigthTool.mel` example can be found in the scripts directory.

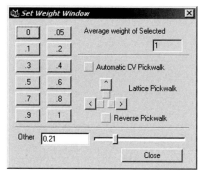

The weightTool window using a formLayout

Here is its simplified source code:

```
global proc makeweightWin(string $window)
{
    window -title "Set Weight Window"
            -iconName "Weight Window" -titleBar true
            -minimizeButton true -maximizeButton false
            -wh 308 260 -s false $window;

    formLayout weightForm;
        button -l "0"   -w 40 a0;
        button -l ".05" -w 40 a05;
        button -l ".1"  -w 40 a1;
        button -l ".2"  -w 40 a2;
        button -l ".3"  -w 40 a3;
        button -l ".4"  -w 40 a4;
        button -l ".5"  -w 40 a5;
        button -l ".6"  -w 40 a6;
        button -l ".7"  -w 40 a7;
        button -l ".8"  -w 40 a8;
        button -l ".9"  -w 40 a9;
        button -l "1"   -w 40 a10;


        text -l "Average weight of Selected" avg;
        textFieldGrp -cw 1 50 -ed false listCVs;


        symbolCheckBox -w 15 -h 15 checkOn;
        symbolCheckBox -w 15 -h 15 checkRev;


        separator -style "in" sep;
        separator -style "in" sep1;
```

```
floatSliderGrp -l "Other" -field true -s 0.01
                        -min 0 -max 1 other;
string $closeButton = `button -l "Close" -w 100
            -c ("window -e -vis 0 " + $window)
            close1`;


button -l "^" -w 20 -h 20 up;
button -l ">" -w 20 -h 20 right;
button -l "<" -w 20 -h 20 left;
symbolCheckBox -w 12 -h 12 upW;
symbolCheckBox -w 12 -h 12 rightW;
symbolCheckBox -w 12 -h 12 leftW;


text -l "Lattice Pickwalk" pw;
text -l "Reverse Pickwalk" revpw;
text -l "Automatic CV Pickwalk" checkOnt;


formLayout -e
    -af a0  "top" 10       -af a0  "left" 10
    -ac a1  "top" 4 a0     -af a1  "left" 10
    -ac a3  "top" 4 a1     -af a3  "left" 10
    -ac a5  "top" 4 a3     -af a5  "left" 10
    -ac a7  "top" 4 a5     -af a7  "left" 10
    -ac a9  "top" 4 a7     -af a9  "left" 10
    -af a05 "top" 10       -ac a05 "left" 10 a0
    -ac a2  "top" 4 a05    -ac a2  "left" 10 a1
    -ac a4  "top" 4 a2     -ac a4  "left" 10 a3
    -ac a6  "top" 4 a4     -ac a6  "left" 10 a5
    -ac a8  "top" 4 a6     -ac a8  "left" 10 a7
    -ac a10 "top" 4 a8     -ac a10 "left" 10 a9
    -ac sep "top" 6 a9     -af sep "left" 10
    -af sep "right" 10
    -ac sep1 "top" 2 listCVs -ac sep1 "left" 10 a10
    -af sep1 "right" 10
    -ac other "top" 15 a9 -af other "right" 10
    -ac checkOn "top" 15 listCVs
    -ac checkOn "left" 20 a2
    -ac checkOnt "top" 15 listCVs
    -ac checkOnt "left" 5 checkOn
    -ac checkRev "top" 5 right
    -ac checkRev "left" 48 a2
    -ac revpw "left" 5 checkRev
    -ac revpw "top" 5 right
```

```
        -af avg "top" 10           -ac avg "left" 20 a05
        -af listCVs "top" 30       -af listCVs "right" 20
        -ac pw "left" 2 right      -ac pw "top" 18 checkOn
        -ac up "left" 45 a10       -ac up "top" 10 checkOn
        -ac upW "left" 50 a10      -ac upW "top" 0 up
        -ac right "left" 70 a10
        -ac right "top" 40 checkOn
        -ac rightW "right" 0 right
        -ac rightW "top" 45 checkOn
        -ac left "left" 20 a10
        -ac left "top" 40 checkOn
        -ac leftW "left" 0 left
        -ac leftW "top" 45 checkOn
        -af close1 "bottom" 8
        -af close1 "right" 20

        weightForm;
    }
global proc weightTool()
{
    string $window = "setWeightWINDOW";
    if (!`window -exists $window`)
        makeweightWin($window);
    showWindow $window;
}
```

Torn-off shelf

This is an example of a `shelfTabLayout` command. In this script, the basic shape of the window is created, then Maya goes to look and see what buttons will be in the window. Some of the commands may not make sense to you at this point, but we will cover most everything in this example by the end of the book.

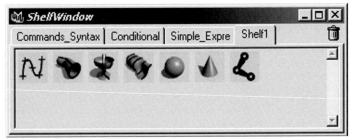

Shelves in a floating window

```
global proc tornOffShelfWindow(string $ShelfWindow)
{
   //Turn save shelf to explicit
   optionVar -iv saveShelfState 1;
   optionVar -iv saveShelfState 0;


   //Initialize our variables
   string $command;
   string $list;
   string $shelves[];


   //Get the shelf directory and get its content
   //depending on Operating System
   if (`about -irix`)
   {
      $command = ("ls \"" + (`getenv "HOME"`) +
            "/maya/5.0/prefs/shelves/*.mel\"");
      $list = `system $command`;
   }
   else if (`about -windows`)
   {
      $command = ("dir /W /ON /B \"" +
            (`getenv "HOME"`) +
            "\\maya\\5.0\\prefs\\shelves\\*.mel\"");
      $command = substituteAllString($command,
                                     "/", "\\");
      $list = `system $command`;
   }
   //Fill our array with the file listing
   tokenize($list, "\n", $shelves);
```

```
//Create the window
window -wh 260 400 $ShelfWindow;

    shelfTabLayout -image "smallTrash.xpm"
                    -imageVisible true mainShelfTab;


for($item in $shelves)
{
    //catch if this string have ".mel" in it
    if(`gmatch $item "*.mel*"`)
    {
        //shortItem is for the proc call
        //buttonLabel is for the tab label
        string $shortItem;
        string $buttonLabel;


        //Use a bunch of substitute command to get
        //the proper name
        //NOTE : ".*" in the command is a wildcard
        //         else it would looks for the
        //          character "*"
        $shortItem = substitute(".mel.*", $item, "");

        $shortItem = substitute(".*shelf_",
                            $shortItem, "shelf_");

        $buttonLabel = substitute("shelf_",
                            $shortItem, "");


        //Make a tab with the good name
        shelfLayout $buttonLabel;


        //Execute the global proc of that shelf
        //This is where all the buttons are created
        eval ($shortItem + "()");


        //Make sure to parent all the buttons to the
        //tab
        setParent ..;
    }
}
```

```
}

global proc tornOffShelf()
{
   //The name of our window
   string $ShelfWindow = "ShelfWindow";
   if(!`window -exists $ShelfWindow`)
   {
      //Launch the proc that will make the window
      tornOffShelfWindow($ShelfWindow);
   }
   showWindow $ShelfWindow;
}
```

B Expressions Appendix

MORE EXPRESSIONS EXAMPLES

Expressions in shaders (Unicycle.ma)

This example reviews expressions used to control shader attributes. Here, we have used two expressions. One to make an object get darker as it moves along the z axis and another to control the rotation of the wheel.

Unicycle before and after

Tip: The `colorR` attribute value is clamped between zero and one and is the portion the `translateZ` attribute value from -12 to 3.

Move the unicycle up and down the z axis to see how the seat color changes. The seat should get darker as it moves backward.

There are two expressions on this unicycle.

UnicycleColor

```
phongE1.colorR = clamp(0, 1, (12 +
                unicycle.translateZ) / 15);
```

UnicycleWheel

```
wheel.rotateX = unicycle.translateZ * 30;
```

Circling (CircularMotion.ma)

In this scene, the *circler* object just moves around in a circle.

An expression variable controls the speed of the object. Also, there are two variables that control the radius of the circle. One is for the radius in the x axis and the other is for the z. This allows you to create an ellipsoidal motion for the object.

```
float $speed = time / 5;
float $xAmplitude = time / 5;
float $zAmplitude = time / 5;


circler.translateX = $xAmplitude *
                              sin($speed * time);
circler.translateZ = $zAmplitude *
                              cos($speed * time);
```

Inward spiral (Spiral.ma)

The trent object moves in a spiral that has a decreasing radius.

The expression contains variables to control the speed of the movement along the spiral, the maximum radius, and the rate at which the object moves inward. The trent object finally hits the center after the 500th frame.

Spiral Motion

```
float $speed = 1;
float $maxRadius = 7;
float $spiralInRate = 0.05;


$maxRadius *= 1 -
              linstep(0, 1, time * $spiralInRate);
trent.translateX = $maxRadius * sin($speed * time);
trent.translateZ = $maxRadius * cos($speed * time);
```

Magnets (Magnets.ma)

The magnets scene is comprised of two objects that have a seemingly magnetic attraction to each other.

In the expression that controls the position of the objects are variables that control certain aspects of the objects' behavior. The main aspects are the initial velocity of the objects and the strength of the attractive force. Other aspects are the damping of the velocity, much like the friction on the objects, and the minimum distance that the magnetization occurs.

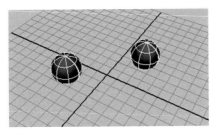

The magnets scene

Magnets Expression

```
float $damping = 0.02;
float $magnitization = 0.1;
float $minimumDistance = 1;


vector $initialVelocity1 = <<0.1, 0.1, -0.1>>;
vector $initialVelocity2 = <<-.1, -0.1, 0.1>>;


global vector $velocity1 = <<0, 0, 0>>;
global vector $velocity2 = <<0, 0, 0>>;


if (frame <= 1)
{
    love.translateX = 5;

    love.translateY = 0;

    love.translateZ = -5;

    hate.translateX = -5;

    hate.translateY = 0;

    hate.translateZ = 5;


    $velocity1 = $initialVelocity1;

    $velocity2 = $initialVelocity2;
}
```

```
vector $distance =
            <<love.translateX - hate.translateX,
              love.translateY - hate.translateY,
              love.translateZ - hate.translateZ>>;
vector $force = <<0, 0, 0>>;


if ($distance > $minimumDistance)
     $force = $magnitization / mag($distance) *
                                  unit($distance);


$velocity1 = (1 - $damping) * ($velocity1 - $force);
$velocity2 = (1 - $damping) * ($velocity2 + $force);


love.translateX += $velocity1.x;
love.translateY += $velocity1.y;
love.translateZ += $velocity1.z;
hate.translateX += $velocity2.x;
hate.translateY += $velocity2.y;
hate.translateZ += $velocity2.z;
```

Perfect bouncing (BouncingElastic.ma)

For this scene, an expression is applied to a super ball making it bounce in a perfect fashion. The ball only bounces straight up and does not have any friction associated with it so it always bounces to the same height. There is a variable in the expression that allows you to change the gravity magnitude that is acting on the super ball.

Bouncing Expression

```
float $gravity = 980; // cm/sec
float $velocity;


superBall.translateY += $velocity / 24; // cm/sec/fps


if (frame <= 1)
{
   superBall.translateY = 10;
   $velocity = 0;
}
```

```
if (superBall.translateY < 0)
    $velocity *= -1;
else
    $velocity -= $gravity / 576;
```

Bouncing (BouncingPlastic.ma)

This scene adds in friction to the perfect bouncing super ball. The super ball bounces lower and lower depending on what the elasticity variable is set to. You can think of elasticity as how bouncy the super ball is.

Bouncing Expression

```
float $gravity = 980; // cm/s
float $elasticity = 0.9;

global float $velocity;

superBall.translateY += $velocity / 24; // 24 fps

if (frame <= 1)
{
    superBall.translateY = 10;
    $velocity = 0;
}


if (superBall.translateY < 0)
    $velocity *= -$elasticity;
else
    $velocity -= $gravity / 576;
```

Wind blown flower (WindyFlowerMoves.ma)

In this scene, a flower's motion is controlled using the handle of an IK spline that has a bind skin on it.

An expression is used here to move the handle using the dnoise function. This allows the motion of the flower to be random and smooth in time. There are variables that allow you to control the amplitude and frequency of the motion of the flower.

The flower moves randomly

Flower Motion Expression

```
float $amplitude = 5;

float $frequency = 0.1;

vector $ikPos = <<ikHandle1.translateX - 10,
                 ikHandle1.translateY - 40,
                 ikHandle1.translateZ>>;


vector $noise = $amplitude * dnoise($ikPos /
                          $amplitude * $frequency +
                          time * <<1, 2, 3>>);


ikHandle1.translateX = 10 + $noise.x;
ikHandle1.translateY = 40 + $noise.y;
ikHandle1.translateZ = $noise.z;
```

Wind rotating a flower (WindyFlowerRotates.ma)

To make the flower move more realistically, rotations of the flower petals were added. The flower motion expression exists on the flower, but now we've added a rotation expression to the petals.

This new expression has variables for controlling the amplitude and frequency of the rotation of the petals.

Making a rock (Rock.ma)

A rock is created from a soft bodied NURBS sphere using an expression that combines `noise` and `dnoise` to set the positions of the soft body particles.

The softbody rock

This expression has variables for the amplitude of the `noise` and `dnoise` components, the frequency, and phase of the sphere distortions. Additionally, there is a variable that allows a fall-off of the distortions so a static state is obtained. Once you have a look of the rock that you like, you can duplicate the rock to keep a copy of that shape.

Rock Expression

```
float $dnoise = 3;
float $noise = 0.3;
float $frequency = 0.3;
float $falloff = 0;
float $phase = 1;

rockParticles.position += $dnoise *
        (dnoise(rockParticles.position * $frequency +
        $phase * <<1, 2, 3>>) + $noise * <<rand(1) -
        0.5, rand(1) - 0.5, rand(1) - 0.5>>) /
        pow(time + 1, $falloff);
```

Bottle bobble (Bobble.ma)

This scene is simply a bottle that is off balance and righting itself. The bottle wobbles around, until it is resting on its base correctly.

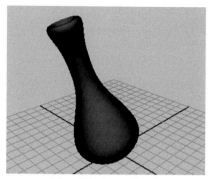

The off balance bottle

There are expression variables that control the start and end times of the bobble as well as the initial rotation values of the bottle. There is also a `noise` multiplier to increase the amount of bobble the bottle experiences.

Bobble Expression

```
// User inputs
// Make sure Rotate pivot is at base of object


float $start = 30;        // start frame of bobble
float $end = 200;         // last frame of bobble
float $startRotateX = -20; // rotation start values
float $startRotateZ = 25;  // rotation start values
float $noiseMult = 5;     // noise: 0 none, + more

float $noise = noise(time) * $noiseMult;
float $ramp = smoothstep($start, $end, frame);

bottle.rotateX = ( sin( time * 4 * pow(5, $ramp) ) *
          $startRotateX + $noise) * (1 - $ramp);

bottle.rotateZ = ( cos( time * 4 * pow(5, $ramp) ) *
          $startRotateZ + $noise) * (1 - $ramp);
```

Bully bullies (Bullies.ma)

The following scene uses an expression in which the position of several spheres influence the position of the cone. This expression illustrates how to use and control multiple attributes in a single expression. Although the only attributes controlled in this expression are the translate attributes of the cone, the expression could have controlled any number of attributes in the scene and not just the ones on the cone.

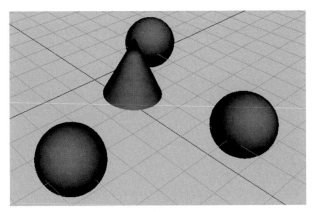

The bullies scene

In this scene, the motion of the spheres was keyframed over 400 frames. The motion of the cone is controlled through an expression that takes into account the positions of all the spheres.

To interactively explore the resultant cone behavior, switch to the top view and manually move the spheres around. (The top view is used to keep all of the objects in the xz plane which makes what is happening easier to visualize.) The expression will be evaluated based on the positions of the spheres and the cone will move as you move the spheres.

Bullies

```
float $speed = 0.1;
float $distance = 4;

vector $position = <<nurbsCone1.translateX,
                     nurbsCone1.translateY,
                     nurbsCone1.translateZ>>;

vector $adversary1 = <<nurbsSphere1.translateX,
                       nurbsSphere1.translateY,
                       nurbsSphere1.translateZ>>;

vector $adversary2 = <<nurbsSphere2.translateX,
                       nurbsSphere2.translateY,
                       nurbsSphere2.translateZ>>;

vector $adversary3 = <<nurbsSphere3.translateX,
                       nurbsSphere3.translateY,
                       nurbsSphere3.translateZ>>;
```

```
vector $toAd1 = $adversary1 - $position;
vector $toAd2 = $adversary2 - $position;
vector $toAd3 = $adversary3 - $position;
vector $move = 0;


if ($toAd1 < $toAd2)
{
   if ($toAd3 < $toAd1)
      $move = unit($toAd3) * $speed * (mag($toAd3) -
                                          $distance);
   else
      $move = unit($toAd1) * $speed * (mag($toAd1) -
                                          $distance);
}
else
{
   if ($toAd3 < $toAd2)
      $move = unit($toAd3) * $speed * (mag($toAd3) -
                                          $distance);
   else
      $move = unit($toAd2) * $speed * (mag($toAd2) -
                                          $distance);
}


nurbsCone1.translateX += $move.x;
nurbsCone1.translateY += $move.y;
nurbsCone1.translateZ += $move.z;
```

Play ball (PlayingBall.ma)

As a glimpse into the potential of using expressions, this scene incorporates a simple artificial intelligence into two characters playing ball. The left character picks up the ball, shakes it sideways, then puts it down at a certain location. Then the right character picks up the ball, shakes it up and down, then puts it down. At that ball location, the left character goes to pick up the ball again, repeating the process.

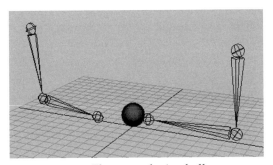

The arms playing ball

Melbots artificial intelligence (Melbots.ma)

Here is an even more complex example of expression driven artificial intelligence. This scene is basically just two rigid bodies moving with dynamics, but the expressions make then move *logically*. The expressions also let you customize certain aspects of the dynamics of the robot.

You can play or render the scene over and over and the results will always be different. If you want a little more challenge, try creating your own robot and make it move with dynamics.

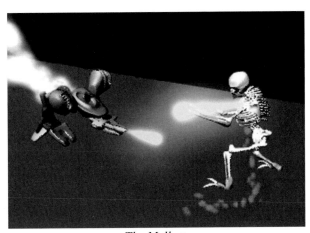

The Melbots

The potential for using expressions to access and modify multiple attributes of numerous objects is limitless. You can create anything from complex relationships between scene elements to beings with artificial intelligence. The hardest part of doing this can be just broadening your awareness of all that can be accomplished using this technique.

Want to Learn More?

Alias|Wavefront publishes a variety of self-study learning materials that can help you improve your skills.

Visit

www.aliaswavefrontstore.com

and check out our books and training materials.